JUMBLE®
BrainBusters
IV
The Adventure Continues

David L. Hoyt and Russell L. Hoyt

TRIUMPH BOOKS
CHICAGO

This book is available in quantity at special discounts
for your group or organization.

For further information, contact:

Triumph Books
814 North Franklin Street
Chicago, Illinois 60610

ISBN 978-1-57243-489-9

Printed in the United States of America

CONTENTS

JUMBLE®

BrainBusters

BEGINNER PUZZLES

ALL ABOUT MUSIC

Unscramble the Jumbles, one letter to each square, to spell words related to music.

#1 BOEO

#2 APION

#3 BJONA

#4 OVINIL

#5 TAURIG

#6 CEORCNT

Box of Clues

Stumped? Maybe you can find a clue below.

- Electric _____
- Single-reed woodwind instrument having a cylindrical tube
- Grand _____
- Musical instrument with a drumlike body and fretted neck
- Double-reed woodwind instrument having a conical tube
- String instrument that dates back hundreds of years
- Musical performance

Arrange the circled letters to solve the mystery answer.

MYSTERY ANSWER

JUMBLE TRIVIA

Unscramble the Jumbles, one letter to each square, to spell words as suggested by the trivia clues.

#1 This country is home to more lakes than all other countries combined.

#1 DANAAC

#2 It takes about 40 days for an _____ egg to hatch.

#2 CTOISRH

#3 This performer appeared in a Southern Maid Doughnuts TV commercial that ran in 1954.

#3 YSREEPL

#4 Joshua Pusey of Pennsylvania received a patent for a book of these in 1892.

#4 CHATESM

#5 This is about three times the size of Texas.

#5 ANREGEDNL

Arrange the circled letters to solve the mystery answer.

This opened for business in 1955.

MYSTERY ANSWER

MOVIES

JUMBLE BrainBusters

Unscramble the Jumbles, one letter to each square, to spell names of movies.

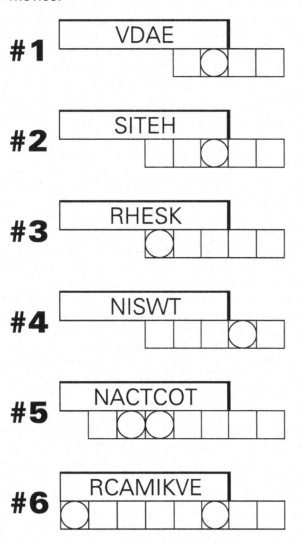

#1 VDAE

#2 SITEH

#3 RHESK

#4 NISWT

#5 NACTCOT

#6 RCAMIKVE

Box of Clues

Stumped? Maybe you can find a clue below.

- 1997 Jodie Foster movie
- 1993 Kevin Kline, Sigourney Weaver movie
- 2001 movie about a reclusive ogre
- 2001 Gene Hackman, Danny DeVito movie
- 2002 Al Pacino, Robin Williams movie
- 1988 Arnold Schwarzenegger, Danny DeVito movie
- 1994 Mel Gibson, Jodie Foster movie

MYSTERY ANSWER

Arrange the circled letters to solve the mystery answer.

ANIMALS

JUMBLE
BrainBusters

Unscramble the Jumbles, one letter to each square, to spell names of animals.

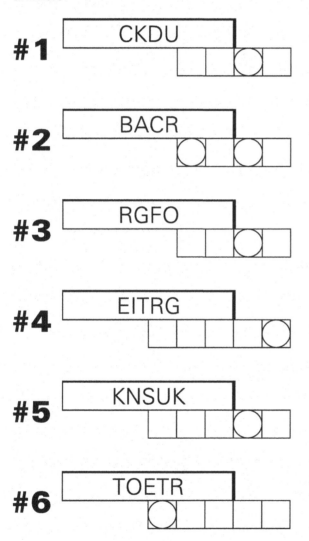

#1 CKDU

#2 BACR

#3 RGFO

#4 EITRG

#5 KNSUK

#6 TOETR

Interesting Animal Facts

An adult jackrabbit can leap about 20 feet in a single bound.

Sturgeon can live as long as 100 years.

A baby blue whale is about 25-feet long at birth.

Arrange the circled letters to solve the mystery answer.

MYSTERY ANSWER

RHYMING WORDS

JUMBLE BrainBusters

Unscramble the Jumbles, one letter to each square, to spell pairs of words that rhyme.

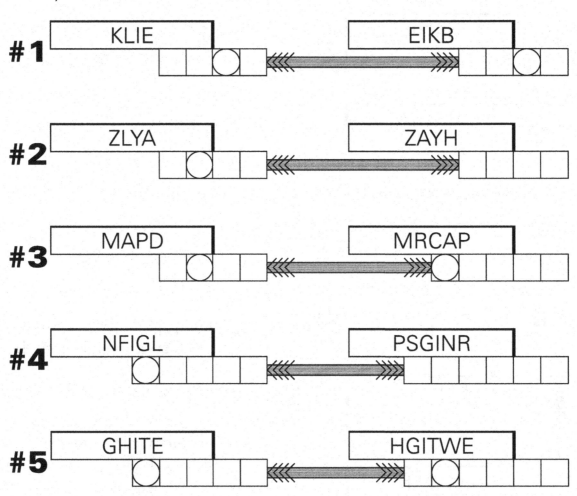

#1 KLIE — EIKB

#2 ZLYA — ZAYH

#3 MAPD — MRCAP

#4 NFIGL — PSGINR

#5 GHITE — HGITWE

Arrange the circled letters to solve the mystery answer.
(Form two words that rhyme.)

MYSTERY ANSWER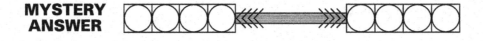

U.S. STATES

JUMBLE BrainBusters

Unscramble the Jumbles, one letter to each square, to spell names of U.S. states.

#1 AOIW

#2 DIOHA

#3 AMIEN

#4 SAALAK

#5 DEAANV

#6 RAKEBSAN

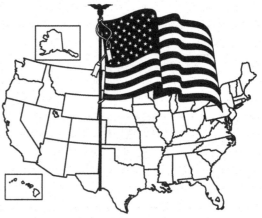

Box of Clues

Stumped? Maybe you can find a clue below.

-Home to part of Hells Canyon
-Largest New England state
-Home to Des Moines
-Home to Mt. McKinley
-U.S. state that borders the Gulf of Mexico
-Home to Carson City
-Home to Lincoln

Arrange the circled letters to solve the mystery answer.

MYSTERY ANSWER

TV SHOWS

JUMBLE
BrainBusters

Unscramble the Jumbles, one letter to each square, to spell names of TV shows.

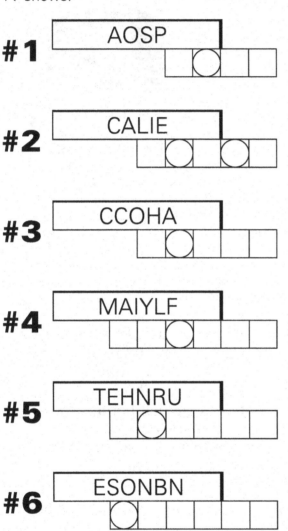

#1 AOSP

#2 CALIE

#3 CCOHA

#4 MAIYLF

#5 TEHNRU

#6 ESONBN

Box of Clues

Stumped? Maybe you can find a clue below.

- ABC drama, 1976-1980
- Controversial ABC sitcom, 1977-1981
- Long-running P.F. show
- CBS sitcom set in Phoenix
- NBC police drama starring Fred Dryer
- ABC sitcom, 1989-1997
- Robert Guillaume sitcom

Arrange the circled letters to solve the mystery answer.

MYSTERY ANSWER

STARTS WITH B

JUMBLE BrainBusters

Unscramble the Jumbles, one letter to each square, to spell words that start with *B*.

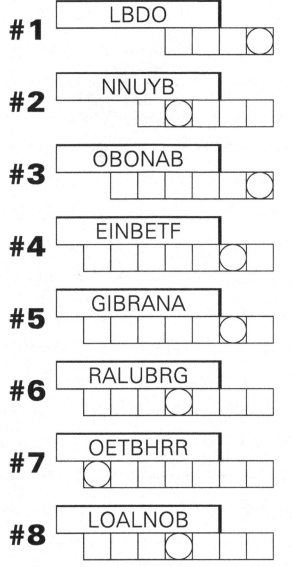

#1 LBDO

#2 NNUYB

#3 OBONAB

#4 EINBETF

#5 GIBRANA

#6 RALUBRG

#7 OETBHRR

#8 LOALNOB

Arrange the circled letters to solve the mystery answer.

B B B B B B
B B B B B B
B B B B B B
B B B B B B

Box of Clues

Stumped? Maybe you can find a clue below.

-Rabbit
-Good deal
-Brave
-Structure
-Bag of lighter-than-air material
-Type of primate
-Something that promotes well-being
-Male sibling
-_____ alarm

MYSTERY ANSWER

OUTER SPACE

Unscramble the Jumbles, one letter to each square, to spell words related to outer space.

#1 OIRTB

#2 MOECT

#3 ANLTPE

#4 STNRAU

#5 XAGAYL

Box of Clues

Stumped? Maybe you can find a clue below.

-The Milky Way or Andromeda
-Home to the "Great Red Spot"
-Sixth planet
-Planet that shares its name with a heavy metallic element
-Mars' designation
-Tailed celestial body
-Encircling motion

#6 TEJIRPU

Arrange the circled letters to solve the mystery answer.

MYSTERY ANSWER

ELEMENTS

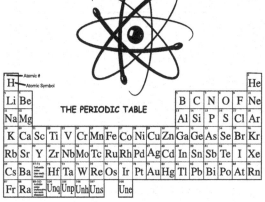

JUMBLE BrainBusters

THE PERIODIC TABLE

Unscramble the Jumbles, one letter to each square, to spell names of elements.

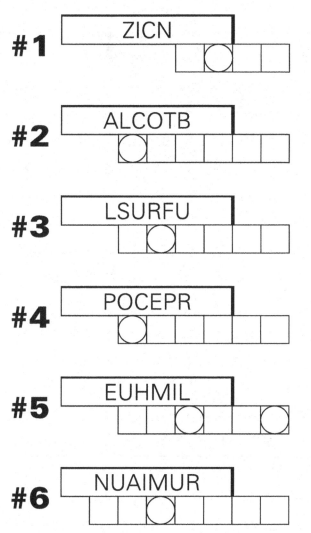

#1 ZICN

#2 ALCOTB

#3 LSURFU

#4 POCEPR

#5 EUHMIL

#6 NUAIMUR

Box of Clues

Stumped? Maybe you can find a clue below.

- Starts with *U*; ends with *M*
- Starts with *C*; ends with *R*
- Starts with *C*; ends with *M*
- Starts with *Z*; ends with *C*
- Starts with *C*; ends with *T*
- Starts with *S*; ends with *R*
- Starts with *H*; ends with *M*

Arrange the circled letters to solve the mystery answer.

MYSTERY ANSWER

AUTOMOBILES

Unscramble the Jumbles, one letter to each square, to spell words related to automobiles.

#1 NENIEG

#2 BCHUAP

#3 TCUHCL

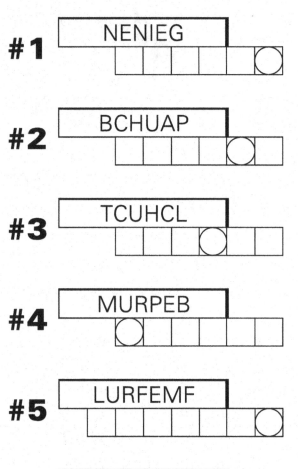

#4 MURPEB

#5 LURFEMF

Box of Clues

Stumped? Maybe you can find a clue below. (No clue for the mystery answer.)

- Sound reducer
- Removable cover
- Front or rear shock absorber
- Extended _____
- Power generator
- Manual transmission part

#6 RTWRAYNA

Arrange the circled letters to solve the mystery answer.

MYSTERY ANSWER

SPORTS

JUMBLE BrainBusters

Unscramble the Jumbles, one letter to each square, to spell words related to sports.

#1 HFITG

#2 PRIELT

#3 GNININ

#4 NTIENS

#5 CHOYKE

#6 BFMEUL

Box of Clues

Stumped? Maybe you can find a clue below.

-Bout
-Field _____
-Football mistake
-Baseball hit
-Baseball increment
-At bat, in baseball
-Table _____

Arrange the circled letters to solve the mystery answer.

MYSTERY ANSWER

AROUND THE HOME

Unscramble the Jumbles, one letter to each square, to spell words related to the home.

#1 TEVN

#2 RFOLO

#3 RTNAYP

#4 DIWNWO

#5 ENHIYCM

#6 BEAMESTN

Box of Clues

Stumped? Maybe you can find a clue below. (No clue for the mystery answer.)

- Starts with *W*; ends with *W*
- Starts with *V*; ends with *T*
- Starts with *P*; ends with *Y*
- Starts with *F*; ends with *R*
- Starts with *C*; ends with *Y*
- Starts with *B*; ends with *T*

Arrange the circled letters to solve the mystery answer.

MYSTERY ANSWER

STARTS WITH A VOWEL

JUMBLE.
BrainBusters

Unscramble the Jumbles, one letter to each square, to spell words that start with a vowel.

#1 EAXP

#2 NGAIA

#3 CEETJ

#4 DIVANE

#5 RIYJUN

#6 ROEFTF

#7 OICTNA

#8 NGUETR

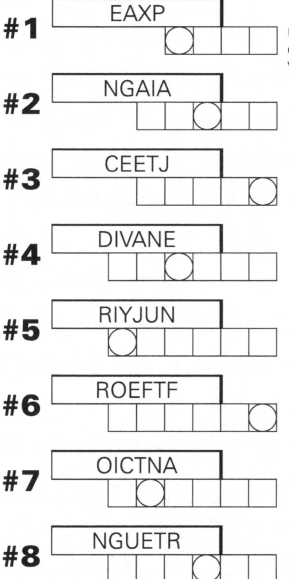

Box of Clues

Stumped? Maybe you can find a clue below.

-Physical damage
-Once more
-Exertion of power
-Throw out
-Energize, bring to life
-Calling for immediate attention
-Summit, tip
-_____ figure
-Enter for conquest

Arrange the circled letters to solve the mystery answer.

MYSTERY ANSWER

PLANET EARTH

JUMBLE BrainBusters

Unscramble the Jumbles, one letter to each square, to spell words related to planet Earth.

#1 EIVRR

#2 CEHBA

#3 MWAPS

#4 NREHTC

#5 NRGUDO

#6 NOLACOV

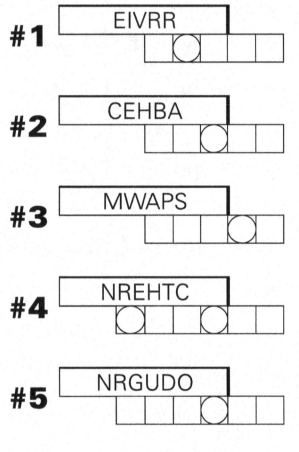

Box of Clues

Stumped? Maybe you can find a clue below.

- Long, narrow, and usually steep-sided depression in the ocean floor
- Explosive vent
- Wetland, often partially or intermittently covered with water
- Projecting landmass
- Flowing body of water
- Shoreline area
- Surface of the Earth

Arrange the circled letters to solve the mystery answer.

MYSTERY ANSWER

RIDDLE RHYME

JUMBLE BrainBusters

Unscramble the Jumbles, one letter to each square, to spell words found in the riddle rhyme.

#1 MYEATSPN

#2 ENOSOR

#3 KAEMS

#4 EYSA

#5 TOFATUENR

by Kim E. Nolan

Car _____ #1 and insurance
Utilities and rent
The quicker you earn it
The _____ #2 it's spent
You can't take it with you
It _____ #3 the world go 'round
It's not _____ #4 to earn
It seldom is found
It's the root of all evil
It won't grow on a tree
Isn't it _____ #5 . . .
The best things are free?

Arrange the circled letters to solve the mystery answer. (The mystery answer is not in the riddle rhyme.)

MYSTERY ANSWER

DOUBLE JUMBLE® BRAINBUSTERS

Unscramble the Jumbles, one letter to each square, to spell words.

#1 ASLBT
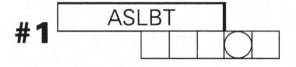

#2 EECAP

#3 UOCTN

#4 CNHHU

#5 MAUNH

#6 TOMOTB

MYSTERY ANSWER #1 SUNNY
MYSTERY ANSWER #2 WEATHER

MYSTERY ANSWER #1 SPORTS
MYSTERY ANSWER #2 ATHLETES

MYSTERY ANSWER #1 COUNTRY
MYSTERY ANSWER #2 ETHIOPIA

Box of Clues

Stumped? Maybe you can find a clue below. (No clues for the mystery answers.)

-Person
-Fun time
-_____ sign
-The South Pole, for example
-Dracula designation
-Intuitive feeling

Arrange the diamonded letters to solve mystery answer #1. Arrange the circled letters to solve mystery answer #2.
(The mystery answers will relate to each other.)

MYSTERY ANSWER #1

MYSTERY ANSWER #2

MEANS THE OPPOSITE

JUMBLE
BrainBusters

Unscramble the Jumbles, one letter to each square, to spell pairs of words that have opposite or nearly opposite meanings.

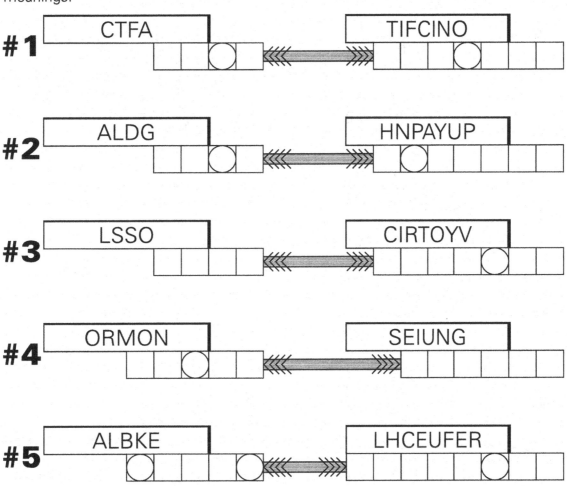

#1 CTFA — TIFCINO

#2 ALDG — HNPAYUP

#3 LSSO — CIRTOYV

#4 ORMON — SEIUNG

#5 ALBKE — LHCEUFER

Arrange the circled letters to solve the mystery answer.
(Form two words that have the opposite or nearly opposite meanings.)

**MYSTERY
ANSWER**

ENDS IN Y

Unscramble the Jumbles, one letter to each square, to spell words that end in Y.

#1 NHIYS

#2 LABYM

#3 GMTYIH

#4 LEMOYD

#5 ERONYJU

#6 DOCSTYU

Arrange the circled letters to solve the mystery answer.

Box of Clues

Stumped? Maybe you can find a clue below.

-Strong
-Lustrous
-Trip
-Roundup
-Guardianship
-Mild
-Song

MYSTERY ANSWER

ALL ABOUT MONEY

Unscramble the Jumbles, one letter to each square, to spell words related to money.

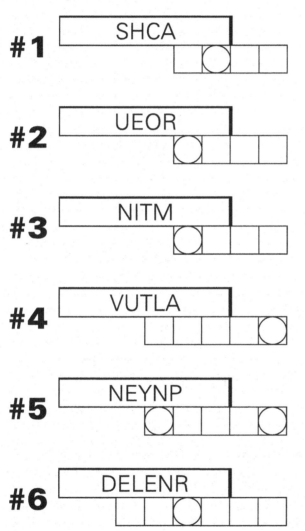

#1 SHCA

#2 UEOR

#3 NITM

#4 VUTLA

#5 NEYNP

#6 DELENR

Box of Clues

Stumped? Maybe you can find a clue below.

-Coin factory
-Copper-colored coin
-Ready money
-European currency
-_____ plan
-Large safe
-Mortgage holder

Arrange the circled letters to solve the mystery answer.

MYSTERY ANSWER

FOOD

JUMBLE BrainBusters

Unscramble the Jumbles, one letter to each square, to spell words related to food.

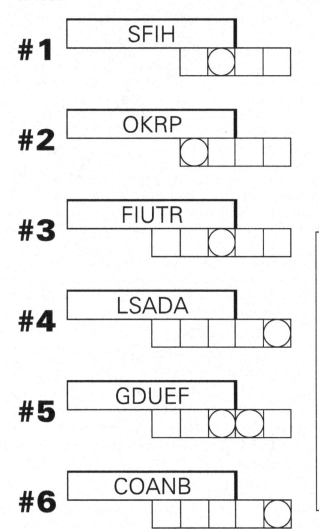

#1 SFIH

#2 OKRP

#3 FIUTR

#4 LSADA

#5 GDUEF

#6 COANB

Box of Clues

Stumped? Maybe you can find a clue below.

-Starts with *B*; ends with *N*
-Starts with *P*; ends with *K*
-Starts with *F*; ends with *H*
-Starts with *F*; ends with *T*
-Starts with *P*; ends with *G*
-Starts with *S*; ends with *D*
-Starts with *F*; ends with *E*

Arrange the circled letters to solve the mystery answer.

MYSTERY ANSWER

WEATHER

JUMBLE BrainBusters

Unscramble the Jumbles, one letter to each square, to spell words related to weather.

#1 RWMA

#2 USLSH

#3 DARAR

Box of Clues

Stumped? Maybe you can find a clue below.

- Wintry mess
- Mild
- Doppler _____
- Partly _____
- Tornado nickname
- Relative _____
- Blustery

#4 DWIYN

#5 LYCUDO

#6 ETIRWTS

Arrange the circled letters to solve the mystery answer.

MYSTERY ANSWER

U.S. STATE CAPITALS

Unscramble the Jumbles, one letter to each square, to spell names of U.S. state capitals.

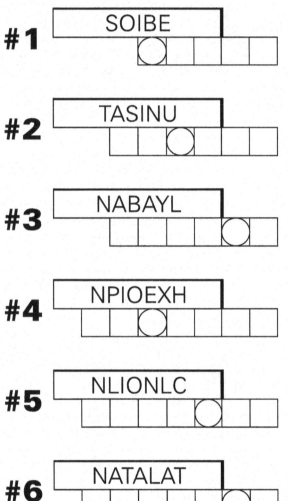

#1 SOIBE

#2 TASINU

#3 NABAYL

#4 NPIOEXH

#5 NLIONLC

#6 NATALAT

Box of Clues

Stumped? Maybe you can find a clue below.

- Capital of the "Cornhusker State"
- Capital of the "Peach State"
- Capital of the "Empire State"
- Capital of the "Grand Canyon State"
- Capital of the "Bay State"
- Capital of the "Lone Star State"
- Capital of the "Gem State"

Arrange the circled letters to solve the mystery answer.

MYSTERY ANSWER

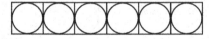

OCCUPATIONS

Unscramble the Jumbles, one letter to each square, to spell names of occupations.

#1 HFCE

#2 PLTIO

#3 CCOHA

#4 OTDROC

#5 TEWIRA

#6 TJONIRA

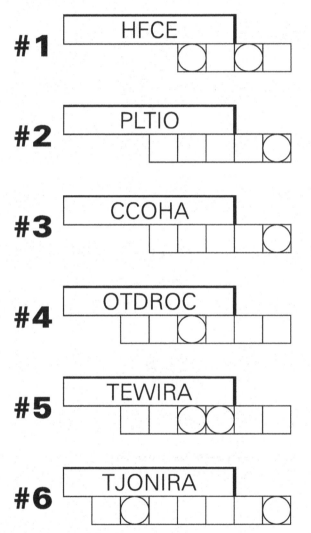

Box of Clues

Stumped? Maybe you can find a clue below.

-Starts with *D*; ends with *R*
-Starts with *C*; ends with *F*
-Starts with *J*; ends with *R*
-Starts with *C*; ends with *H*
-Starts with *W*; ends with *R*
-Starts with *A*; ends with *T*
-Starts with *P*; ends with *T*

Arrange the circled letters to solve the mystery answer.

MYSTERY ANSWER

ADJECTIVES

JUMBLE BrainBusters

Unscramble the Jumbles, one letter to each square, to spell adjectives.

#1 LULD

#2 NALIP

#3 LNOEB

#4 MOYRO

#5 PTDUIS

#6 HRGITB

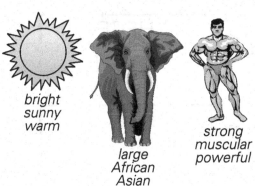

bright
sunny
warm

large
African
Asian

strong
muscular
powerful

Box of Clues

Stumped? Maybe you can find a clue below.

-Spacious
-Smart or luminous
-Glorious, gorgeous, magnificent
-Lackluster, lifeless
-Inelaborate, modest, simple
-Dumb
-Princely, stately, eminent, illustrious

Arrange the circled letters to solve the mystery answer.

MYSTERY ANSWER

COUNTRIES

JUMBLE BrainBusters

Unscramble the Jumbles, one letter
to each square, to spell names of
countries.

#1 DIAIN

#2 APJAN

#3 PEYTG

#4 ZARLIB

#5 NCFAER

#6 ANPLDO

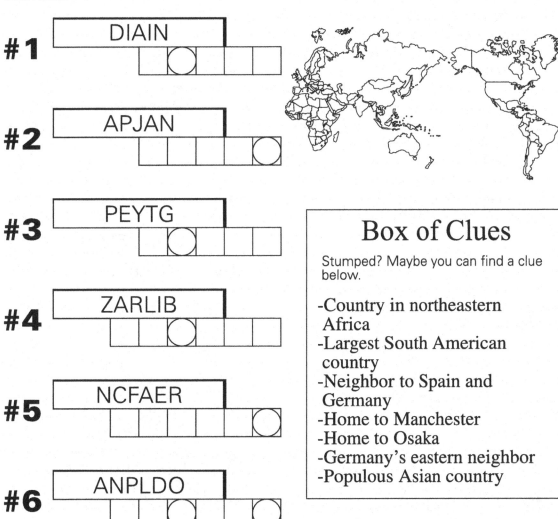

Box of Clues

Stumped? Maybe you can find a clue
below.

-Country in northeastern
 Africa
-Largest South American
 country
-Neighbor to Spain and
 Germany
-Home to Manchester
-Home to Osaka
-Germany's eastern neighbor
-Populous Asian country

Arrange the circled letters
to solve the mystery answer.

MYSTERY ANSWER

THE HUMAN BODY

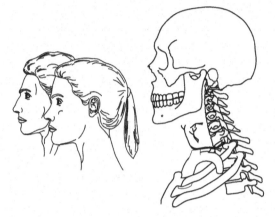

Unscramble the Jumbles, one letter to each square, to spell words related to the human body.

#1 AHED

#2 CENK

#3 NLGU

#4 OFOT

#5 MUHBT

#6 UTOHM

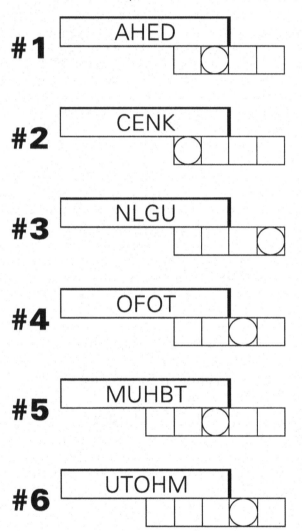

Interesting Human Body Facts

The skeleton of an average 160-pound human body weighs about 29 pounds.

The average human brain comprises about 2 percent of total body weight.

The average human eye can distinguish about 500 different shades of gray.

Arrange the circled letters to solve the mystery answer.

MYSTERY ANSWER

U.S. PRESIDENTS

Unscramble the Jumbles, one letter to each square, to spell the last names of U.S. presidents.

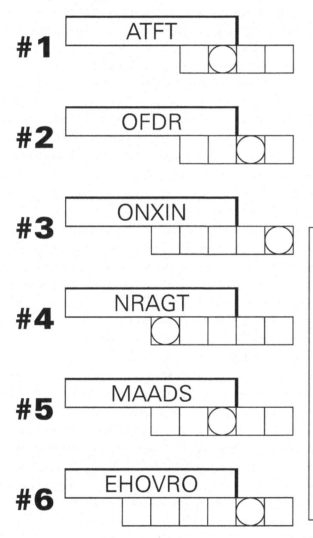

#1 ATFT

#2 OFDR

#3 ONXIN

#4 NRAGT

#5 MAADS

#6 EHOVRO

Arrange the circled letters to solve the mystery answer.

Interesting Presidential Facts

President Ulysses S. Grant was arrested during his term of office. He was convicted of exceeding the speed limit in Washington on his horse and was fined $20.

President William H. Taft was offered a contract to pitch for the Cincinnati Reds.

MYSTERY ANSWER

DOUBLE JUMBLE® BRAINBUSTERS

Unscramble the Jumbles, one letter to each square, to spell words.

#1 NEYPN

#2 CTEHF

#3 GHNITK

#4 SERTJE

#5 ETFRHA

#6 ORANWR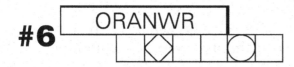

JUMBLE BrainBusters

MYSTERY ANSWER #1 SUNNY
MYSTERY ANSWER #2 WEATHER

MYSTERY ANSWER #1 SPORTS
MYSTERY ANSWER #2 ATHLETES

MYSTERY ANSWER #1 COUNTRY
MYSTERY ANSWER #2 ETHIOPIA

Box of Clues

Stumped? Maybe you can find a clue below. (No clues for the mystery answers.)

-_____-minded
-Retrieve
-Fool
-Pop
-_____ arcade
-Chess piece

Arrange the diamonded letters to solve mystery answer #1. Arrange the circled letters to solve mystery answer #2. (The mystery answers will relate to each other.)

MYSTERY ANSWER #1

MYSTERY ANSWER #2

MEANS THE SAME

JUMBLE BrainBusters

Unscramble the Jumbles, one letter
to each square, to spell pairs of words
that have the same or similar meanings.

#1 SHPU — PIELM

#2 ORWG — NAEXDP

#3 RAHM — GADAEM

#4 AIBCS — RMPIAYR

#5 UTRBLA — AEASGV

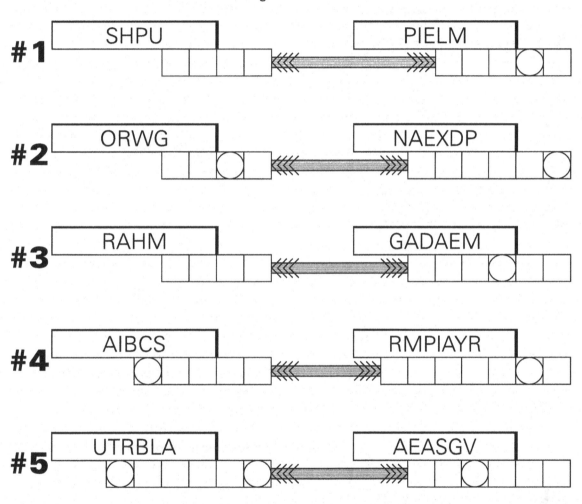

Arrange the circled letters to solve the mystery answer.
(Form two words that have the same or similar meanings.)

**MYSTERY
ANSWER**

ANIMALS

JUMBLE
BrainBusters

Unscramble the Jumbles, one letter to each square, to spell names of animals.

#1 SIFH

#2 OMEL

#3 EELGA

#4 ALHEW

#5 LETRUT

#6 KEHICNC

Box of Clues

Stumped? Maybe you can find a clue below.

-Powerful bird of prey
-Grouper or salmon
-Largest creature on Earth
-Slow-moving reptile
-Fast feline
-One of the most widely domesticated poultry species
-Burrowing insectivore

Arrange the circled letters to solve the mystery answer.

MYSTERY ANSWER

GOLF

JUMBLE BrainBusters

Unscramble the Jumbles, one letter to each square, to spell words related to golf.

#1 SIECL

#2 LAEEG

#3 EVRIRD

#4 RAADHZ

#5 LPARME

#6 MNAONR

Box of Clues

Stumped? Maybe you can find a clue below. (No clue for the mystery answer.)

-Long club
-Water _____
-Greg _____
-Arnold _____
-Type of bad shot
-A score of 3 on a par 5

MYSTERY ANSWER

Arrange the circled letters to solve the mystery answer.

TV SHOWS

JUMBLE BrainBusters

Unscramble the Jumbles, one letter to each square, to spell names of TV shows.

#1 UDMEA

#2 EEILRM

#3 EEBKRC

#4 ERCESH

#5 PLFIRPE

#6 RHNEAWT

Box of Clues

Stumped? Maybe you can find a clue below.

- NBC sitcom set in Boston
- The number two show on TV during the 1964–1965 season
- CBS sitcom starring T.D.
- An *All In the Family* spin-off
- CBS sitcom set in Vermont
- Short-lived sitcom about a chef
- NBC show starring a swimmer

Arrange the circled letters to solve the mystery answer.

MYSTERY ANSWER

FOOD

JUMBLE BrainBusters

Unscramble the Jumbles, one letter to each square, to spell words related to food.

#1 EBFE

#2 ZIPZA

#3 AUGRS

#4 LPICEK

#5 RKUYTE

Box of Clues

Stumped? Maybe you can find a clue below.

-Sweetener
-Cow meat
-American _____
-Thanksgiving bird
-Dill _____
-Sometimes served with gravy
-Sausage _____

#6 EHECES

Arrange the circled letters to solve the mystery answer.

MYSTERY ANSWER

RHYMING WORDS

Unscramble the Jumbles, one letter
to each square, to spell pairs of words
that rhyme.

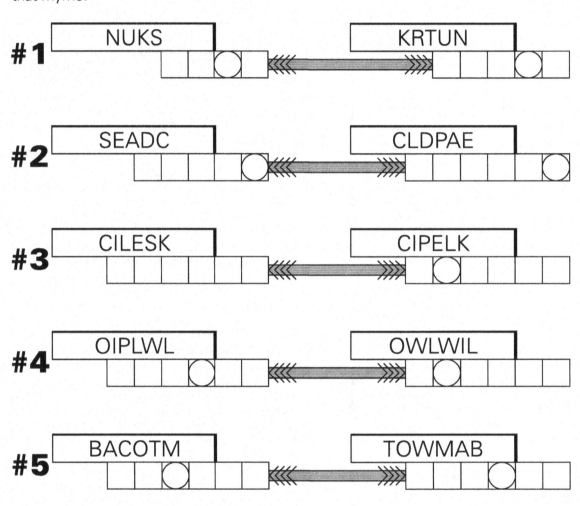

#1 NUKS   KRTUN

#2 SEADC   CLDPAE

#3 CILESK   CIPELK

#4 OIPLWL   OWLWIL

#5 BACOTM   TOWMAB

Arrange the circled letters to solve the mystery answer.
(Form two words that rhyme.)

**MYSTERY
ANSWER**

SPORTS

JUMBLE BrainBusters

Unscramble the Jumbles, one letter to each square, to spell words related to sports.

#1 BUYRG

#2 RRROE

#3 ACOHC

#4 SIGINK

#5 LHETEM

#6 WFIAYAR

Box of Clues

Stumped? Maybe you can find a clue below.

- Starts with *E*; ends with *R*
- Starts with *C*; ends with *H*
- Starts with *R*; ends with *Y*
- Starts with *S*; ends with *G*
- Starts with *U*; ends with *M*
- Starts with *F*; ends with *Y*
- Starts with *H*; ends with *T*

Arrange the circled letters to solve the mystery answer.

MYSTERY ANSWER

DOUBLE JUMBLE® BRAINBUSTERS

Unscramble the Jumbles, one letter to each square, to spell words.

#1 HLITG

#2 LACEB

#3 PEPAR

#4 RAMYR

#5 OTMHU

#6 CIONEM

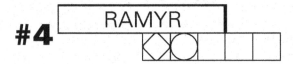

JUMBLE BrainBusters

MYSTERY ANSWER #1 SUNNY
MYSTERY ANSWER #2 WEATHER

MYSTERY ANSWER #1 SPORTS
MYSTERY ANSWER #2 ATHLETES

MYSTERY ANSWER #1 COUNTRY
MYSTERY ANSWER #2 ETHIOPIA

Box of Clues

Stumped? Maybe you can find a clue below. (No clues for the mystery answers.)

-Revenue; _____ tax
-_____ money
-Sun output
-River ending
-_____ TV
-Tie the knot

Arrange the diamonded letters to solve mystery answer #1. Arrange the circled letters to solve mystery answer #2. (The mystery answers will relate to each other.)

MYSTERY ANSWER #1

MYSTERY ANSWER #2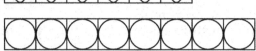

LARGEST OF ITS KIND

JUMBLE BrainBusters

Unscramble the Jumbles, one letter to each square, to spell names of things that are the largest of their kind.

#1 LWAEH

#2 AASALK

#3 RAHAAS

#4 NAACAD

#5 FIACCIP

#6 EJTIRPU

Box of Clues

Stumped? Maybe you can find a clue below.

- Largest body of water on Earth
- Earth's largest desert
- Largest mammal
- Largest planet in the solar system
- Largest living land mammal
- Largest country in North America
- Largest U.S. state

Arrange the circled letters to solve the mystery answer.

MYSTERY ANSWER

POETRY

JUMBLE BrainBusters

Unscramble the Jumbles, one letter to each square, to spell words found in the poem.

#1 NOMNGIR

#2 LJODTE

#3 CUKRT

#4 FIRTD

#5 HOPEN

#6 MBURNE

Noise
by Kim E. Nolan

Early in the ____ #1
The sky is still dark
I am ____ #2 awake
By a dog's awful bark

Next it's the garbage ____ #3
It's two hours early
I must get some sleep
I'm becoming quite surly

As I ____ #4 off, the ____ #5 rings
Again I wake from my slumber
This must be a nightmare
They dialed the wrong ____ #6

Arrange the circled letters
to solve the mystery answer.
(The mystery answer is not
in the poem.)

MYSTERY ANSWER

STARTS WITH G

JUMBLE BrainBusters

Unscramble the Jumbles, one letter to each square, to spell words that start with *G*.

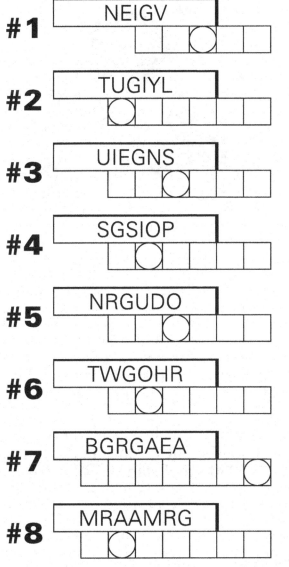

#1 NEIGV

#2 TUGIYL

#3 UIEGNS

#4 SGSIOP

#5 NRGUDO

#6 TWGOHR

#7 BGRGAEA

#8 MRAAMRG

G G G G G G
G G G G G G
G G G G G G
G G G G G G

Box of Clues

Stumped? Maybe you can find a clue below.

-Very smart person
-Chatty talk
-Provided with
-Blameworthy
-_____ school
-Common _____
-Trash
-Lieutenant _____
-Expansion

Arrange the circled letters to solve the mystery answer.

MYSTERY ANSWER

MOVIES

JUMBLE. BrainBusters

Unscramble the Jumbles, one letter to each square, to spell names of movies.

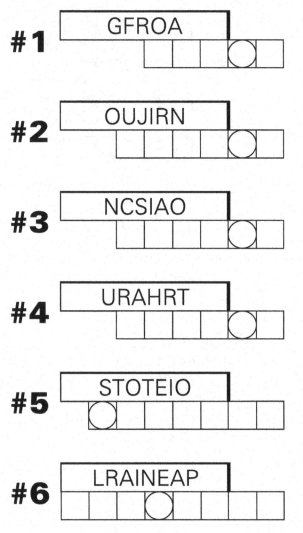

#1 GFROA

#2 OUJIRN

#3 NCSIAO

#4 URAHRT

#5 STOTEIO

#6 LRAINEAP

Box of Clues

Stumped? Maybe you can find a clue below.

- 1981 comedy starring D.M.
- 1996 movie written by the Coen brothers
- 1986 action movie starring T.C.
- 1982 comedy starring D.H.
- 1994 comedy starring A.S.
- 1980 spoof starring R.H. and J.H.
- 1995 drama set in Nevada

Arrange the circled letters to solve the mystery answer.

MYSTERY ANSWER

MATH

JUMBLE
BrainBusters

Unscramble the Jumbled letters, one letter to each square, so that each equation is correct.

For example: NONTEOEOW
ONE + ONE = TWO

#1 VETEIFVFIEN
○ □ □ − □ □ ○ = □ □ □ □

#2 VSISIWEXLETX
□ □ □ □ + □ □ □ □ = □ ○ □ □ □ □

#3 VTNWEEONSIEN
□ ○ □ + □ □ □ □ □ □ = □ □ □ □

#4 RZREOERZOEOZ
□ □ □ ○ + □ □ ○ □ = ○ □ □ □

#5 UEGHFOTUORIRF
□ □ □ □ ○ □ − □ ○ □ □ = □ ○ □ □

Then arrange the circled letters to solve the mystery equation.

MYSTERY EQUATION

○○○ + ○○○○○ = ○○○

OUTER SPACE

Unscramble the Jumbles, one letter to each square, to spell words related to outer space.

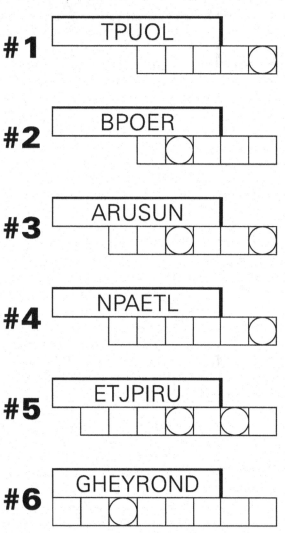

#1 TPUOL

#2 BPOER

#3 ARUSUN

#4 NPAETL

#5 ETJPIRU

#6 GHEYROND

Box of Clues

Stumped? Maybe you can find a clue below. (No clue for the mystery answer.)

-This element is the fuel that powers stars
-Exploratory robot spaceship
-Outermost planet and home to Charon (moon)
-Home to Europa and Io (moons)
-Earth or Venus
-Seventh planet

MYSTERY ANSWER

Arrange the circled letters to solve the mystery answer.

RHYMING WORDS

Unscramble the Jumbles, one letter
to each square, to spell pairs of words
that rhyme.

#1 YUBNN   ENHYO

#2 LCIMA   MAREF

#3 EKANT   NAHESK

#4 MUSERM   EMURBM

#5 ULJEBM   LMUBRCE

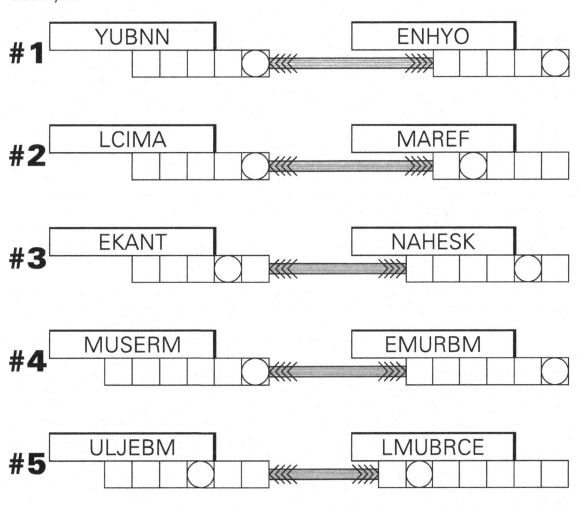

Arrange the circled letters to solve the mystery answer.
(Form two words that rhyme.)

**MYSTERY
ANSWER**

COUNTRIES

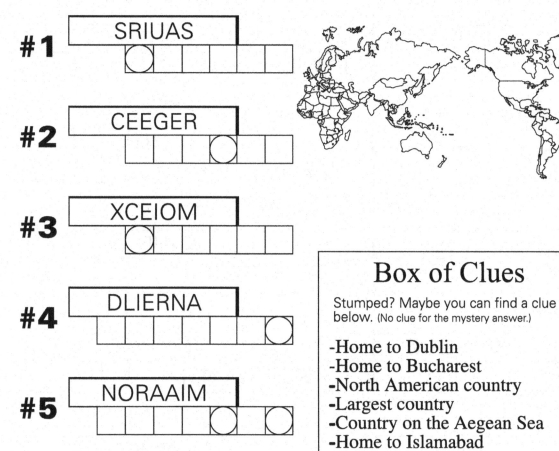

JUMBLE BrainBusters

Unscramble the Jumbles, one letter to each square, to spell names of countries.

#1 SRIUAS

#2 CEEGER

#3 XCEIOM

#4 DLIERNA

#5 NORAAIM

#6 KASPAINT

Box of Clues

Stumped? Maybe you can find a clue below. (No clue for the mystery answer.)

- Home to Dublin
- Home to Bucharest
- North American country
- Largest country
- Country on the Aegean Sea
- Home to Islamabad

Arrange the circled letters to solve the mystery answer.

MYSTERY ANSWER

ALL ABOUT MUSIC

JUMBLE BrainBusters

Unscramble the Jumbles, one letter to each square, to spell words related to music.

#1 CBHA

#2 NOSG

#3 UTFEL

#4 PTOME

#5 LEESATB

#6 PRTMTUE

Box of Clues

Stumped? Maybe you can find a clue below.

- Musical pace
- Grouping of a specified number of musical beats
- "The _____"
- Classical composer
- Keyed woodwind
- Wind instrument consisting of a conical or cylindrical tube
- Tune

Arrange the circled letters to solve the mystery answer.

MYSTERY ANSWER

JUMBLE® TRIVIA

Unscramble the Jumbles, one letter to each square, to spell words as suggested by the trivia clues.

#1 This female figure debuted in 1959.

#1 RIABEB

#2 This animal can move as fast as 30 miles per hour.

#2 ARKNOAOG

#3 The first _____ pens, sold in 1945, were priced at about $12.00 apiece.

#3 NABOLPITL

#4 This man anonymously submitted design plans for the White House, but they were rejected.

#4 ERSJOFENF

#5 The standard _____ moves at a rate of 120 feet per minute.

#5 LSEACORTA

Arrange the circled letters to solve the mystery answer.

This popular song was composed in 1857 by James Pierpont.

MYSTERY ANSWER ⬡⬡⬡⬡⬡⬡ ⬡⬡⬡⬡⬡

FOOD

Unscramble the Jumbles, one letter to each square, to spell words related to food.

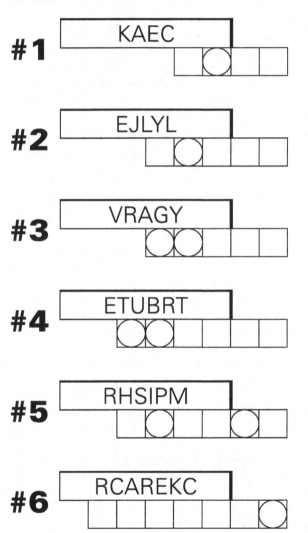

#1 KAEC

#2 EJLYL

#3 VRAGY

#4 ETUBRT

#5 RHSIPM

#6 RCAREKC

Arrange the circled letters to solve the mystery answer.

Interesting Food Facts

In Japan, squid is one of the most popular toppings for pizza.

It takes about one pound of wheat to make three cups of flour.

MYSTERY ANSWER

U.S. STATES

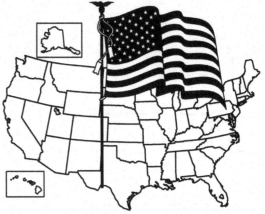

JUMBLE BrainBusters

Unscramble the Jumbles, one letter to each square, to spell names of U.S. states.

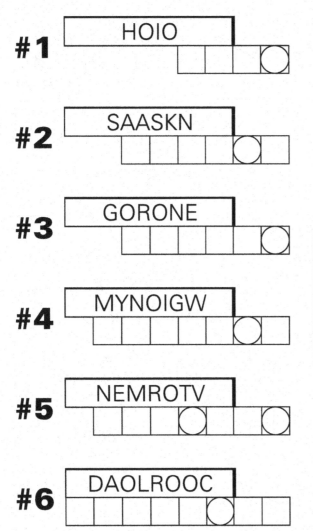

#1 HOIO

#2 SAASKN

#3 GORONE

#4 MYNOIGW

#5 NEMROTV

#6 DAOLROOC

Arrange the circled letters to solve the mystery answer.

Box of Clues

Stumped? Maybe you can find a clue below.

- Starts with *O*; ends with *N*
- Starts with *C*; ends with *O*
- Starts with *O*; ends with *O*
- Starts with *W*; ends with *G*
- Starts with *K*; ends with *S*
- Starts with *M*; ends with *A*
- Starts with *V*; ends with *T*

MYSTERY ANSWER

WEATHER

Unscramble the Jumbles, one letter to each square, to spell words related to weather.

#1 HILA

#2 WOSN

#3 TSOMR

#4 REEDEG

#5 ASRTUST

#6 NWOPOURD

Box of Clues

Stumped? Maybe you can find a clue below.

- Heavy rain
- Wintry precipitation
- Frozen lump
- Clear day's brightness
- Weather disturbance
- Type of cloud
- Temperature unit

Arrange the circled letters to solve the mystery answer.

MYSTERY ANSWER

AUTOMOBILES

Unscramble the Jumbles, one letter to each square, to spell words related to automobiles.

#1 MAREF

#2 CPIPKU

#3 GNENIE

#4 CVEIELH

#5 SHICSSA

Box of Clues

Stumped? Maybe you can find a clue below.

- Starts with *C*; ends with *S*
- Starts with *H*; ends with *S*
- Starts with *O*; ends with *R*
- Starts with *E*; ends with *E*
- Starts with *F*; ends with *E*
- Starts with *P*; ends with *P*
- Starts with *V*; ends with *E*

#6 TOMOERDE

Arrange the circled letters to solve the mystery answer.

MYSTERY ANSWER

DOUBLE JUMBLE® BRAINBUSTERS

Unscramble the Jumbles, one letter to each square, to spell words.

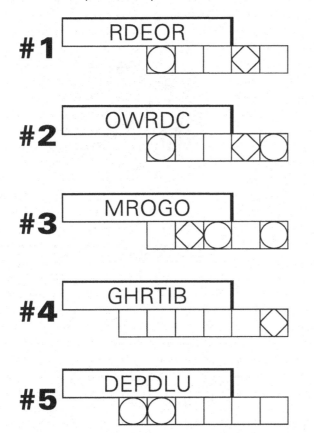

#1 RDEOR

#2 OWRDC

#3 MROGO

#4 GHRTIB

#5 DEPDLU

#6 RNMENA

MYSTERY ANSWER #1 | SUNNY
MYSTERY ANSWER #2 | WEATHER

MYSTERY ANSWER #1 | SPORTS
MYSTERY ANSWER #2 | ATHLETES

MYSTERY ANSWER #1 | COUNTRY
MYSTERY ANSWER #2 | ETHIOPIA

Box of Clues

Stumped? Maybe you can find a clue below. (No clues for the mystery answers.)

-Horde
-Bride's companion
-Request
-Small collection of water
-Method, fashion
-Smart or shining

Arrange the diamonded letters to solve mystery answer #1. Arrange the circled letters to solve mystery answer #2.
(The mystery answers will relate to each other.)

MYSTERY ANSWER #1

MYSTERY ANSWER #2

TV SHOWS

JUMBLE BrainBusters

Unscramble the Jumbles, one letter to each square, to spell names of TV shows.

#1 XITA

#2 ETHLO

#3 FKGNUU

#4 ERRSAIF

#5 ESRARTKT

#6 DGOMTIEOS

Box of Clues

Stumped? Maybe you can find a clue below.

-Sitcom set in N.Y.C., 1978-1983
-A *Maude* spin-off
-ABC Western starring David Carradine
-1960s NBC show set in the future
-A *Cheers* spin-off
-NBC sitcom starring a musical foursome
-ABC drama starring James Brolin

Arrange the circled letters to solve the mystery answer.

MYSTERY ANSWER

BASEBALL

JUMBLE. BrainBusters

Unscramble the Jumbles, one letter to each square, to spell words related to baseball.

#1 VRUEC ◯

#2 ACOHC ◯◯

#3 KTSIER ◯

#4 UODTGU ◯

#5 GNINWRA ◯

#6 ADONDIM ◯

Box of Clues

Stumped? Maybe you can find a clue below. (No clue for the mystery answer.)

- Waiting and watching area
- Type of pitch
- Pitcher's goal
- _____ track
- Bases' shape
- Third-base _____

Arrange the circled letters to solve the mystery answer.

MYSTERY ANSWER

◯◯◯◯◯◯◯

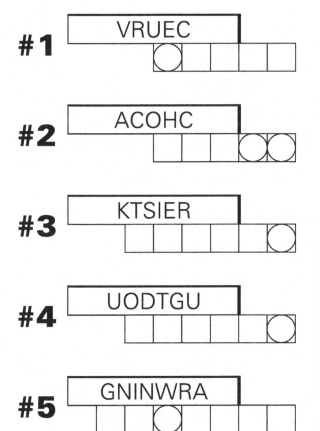

PLANET EARTH

Unscramble the Jumbles, one letter to each square, to spell words related to planet Earth.

#1 VLAA

#2 UFLBF

#3 ASRSG

#4 LEALYV

#5 RTIEWN

#6 GOLANO

Box of Clues

Stumped? Maybe you can find a clue below. (No clue for the mystery answer.)

- High, steep bank
- Shallow sound, channel near a larger body of water
- Depressed area
- Volcano product
- Slender ground cover
- Coldest season

Arrange the circled letters to solve the mystery answer.

MYSTERY ANSWER

ENDS IN Y

Unscramble the Jumbles, one letter to each square, to spell words that end in Y.

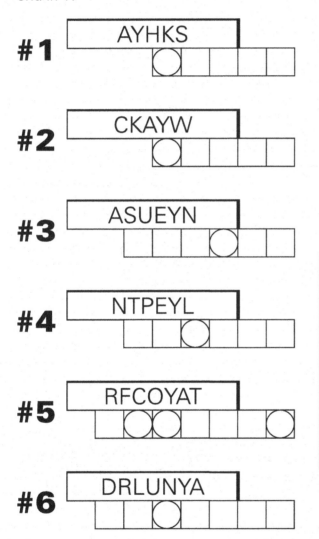

#1 AYHKS

#2 CKAYW

#3 ASUEYN

#4 NTPEYL

#5 RFCOYAT

#6 DRLUNYA

Box of Clues

Stumped? Maybe you can find a clue below. (No clue for the mystery answer.)

-Crazy
-Enough
-Nervous
-Lacking stability
-Manufacturing facility
-_____ room

Arrange the circled letters to solve the mystery answer.

MYSTERY ANSWER

MEANS THE SAME

Unscramble the Jumbles, one letter to each square, to spell pairs of words that have the same or similar meanings.

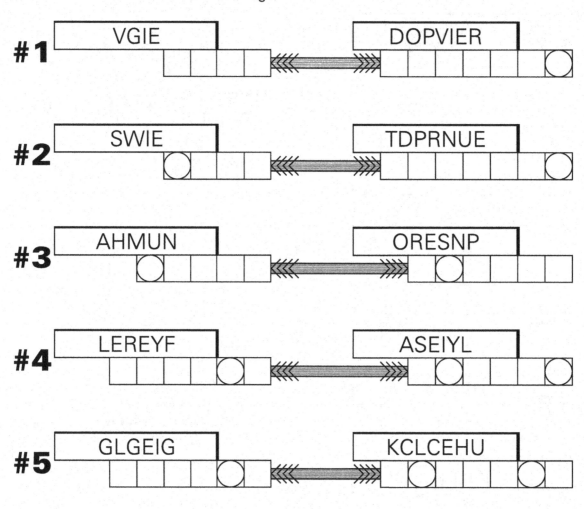

#1 VGIE · DOPVIER

#2 SWIE · TDPRNUE

#3 AHMUN · ORESNP

#4 LEREYF · ASEIYL

#5 GLGEIG · KCLCEHU

Arrange the circled letters to solve the mystery answer.
(Form two words that have the same or similar meanings.)

MYSTERY ANSWER

OCCUPATIONS

Unscramble the Jumbles, one letter to each square, to spell names of occupations.

#1 SRUEN

#2 OAILTR

#3 HATRUO

#4 KERORB

#5 LEROART

#6 BELURPM

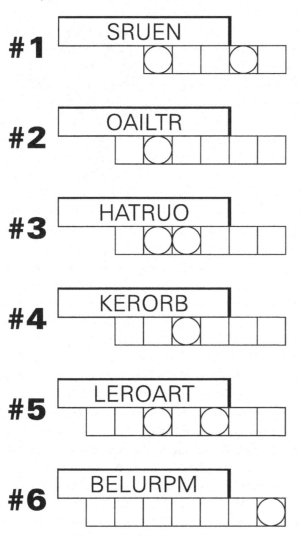

Box of Clues

Stumped? Maybe you can find a clue below.

- Starts with *A*; ends with *R*
- Starts with *R*; ends with *R*
- Starts with *T*; ends with *R*
- Starts with *A*; ends with *T*
- Starts with *P*; ends with *R*
- Starts with *N*; ends with *E*
- Starts with *B*; ends with *R*

Arrange the circled letters to solve the mystery answer.

MYSTERY ANSWER

ANIMALS

Unscramble the Jumbles, one letter to each square, to spell names of animals.

#1 AUPM

#2 NYHAE

#3 MLALA

#4 UOMES

#5 YEUTKR

#6 SRUALW

Box of Clues

Stumped? Maybe you can find a clue below.

-South American pack animal
-Cougar
-Large seal relative
-Slender, nocturnal predator
-Animal that shares its name with a country
-Small rodent
-Doglike carnivore

Arrange the circled letters to solve the mystery answer.

MYSTERY ANSWER

JUMBLE®

BrainBusters

INTERMEDIATE PUZZLES

STARTS WITH A VOWEL

JUMBLE BrainBusters

Unscramble the Jumbles, one letter to each square, to spell words that start with a vowel.

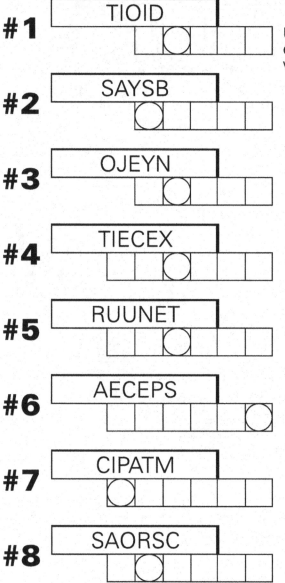

#1 TIOID

#2 SAYSB

#3 OJEYN

#4 TIECEX

#5 RUUNET

#6 AECEPS

#7 CIPATM

#8 SAORSC

Arrange the circled letters to solve the mystery answer.

Box of Clues

Stumped? Maybe you can find a clue below.

-Evade, avoid
-Enthuse
-Bottomless gulf
-Strike forcefully
-Reaching from one side to the other
-False
-Unforeseen and unplanned event
-Take pleasure in
-Moron

MYSTERY ANSWER

U.S. PRESIDENTS

Unscramble the Jumbles, one letter to each square, to spell the last names of U.S. presidents.

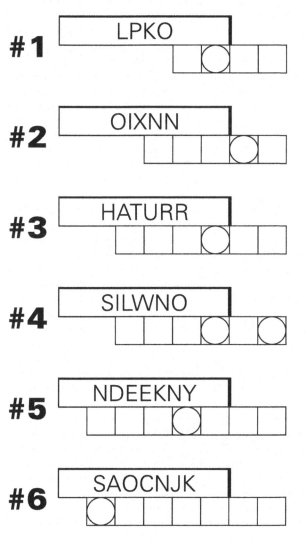

#1 LPKO

#2 OIXNN

#3 HATURR

#4 SILWNO

#5 NDEEKNY

#6 SAOCNJK

Box of Clues

Stumped? Maybe you can find a clue below.

-Chester A. _____
-James K. _____
-28th U.S. president
-35th U.S. president
-17th or 36th U.S. president
-President who shared his last name with the capital of Mississippi
-37th U.S. president

Arrange the circled letters to solve the mystery answer.

MYSTERY ANSWER

ADJECTIVES

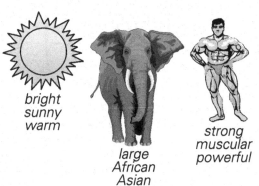

Unscramble the Jumbles, one letter
to each square, to spell adjectives.

#1 NTIY

#2 HFSIY

#3 NADIGR

#4 RODRIH

#5 BFELEE

#6 FJULYO

bright
sunny
warm

large
African
Asian

strong
muscular
powerful

Box of Clues

Stumped? Maybe you can find a clue
below.

-Weak, flimsy
-Dubious, problematic, suspect,
 suspicious, uncertain
-Small
-Bold, courageous
-Glad, happy
-Lesser, lower, subjacent,
 secondary, subordinate
-Ghastly, gruesome

Arrange the circled letters
to solve the mystery answer.

MYSTERY ANSWER

WARS AND THE MILITARY

JUMBLE BrainBusters

Unscramble the Jumbles, one letter to each square, to spell words related to wars and the military.

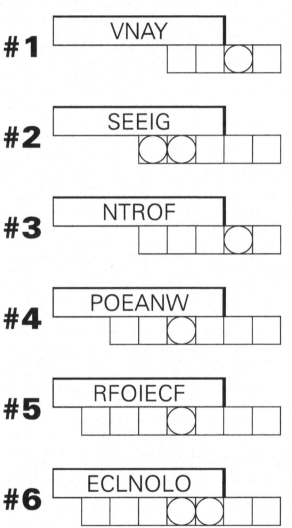

#1 VNAY

#2 SEEIG

#3 NTROF

#4 POEANW

#5 RFOIECF

#6 ECLNOLO

Arrange the circled letters to solve the mystery answer.

MYSTERY ANSWER

MEANS THE OPPOSITE

Unscramble the Jumbles, one letter to each square, to spell pairs of words that have opposite or nearly opposite meanings.

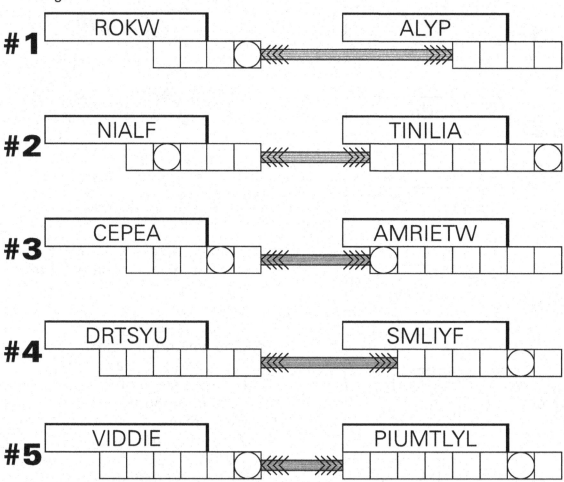

#1 ROKW | ALYP

#2 NIALF | TINILIA

#3 CEPEA | AMRIETW

#4 DRTSYU | SMLIYF

#5 VIDDIE | PIUMTLYL

Arrange the circled letters to solve the mystery answer.
(Form two words that have the opposite or nearly opposite meanings.)

MYSTERY ANSWER

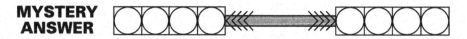

THE HUMAN BODY

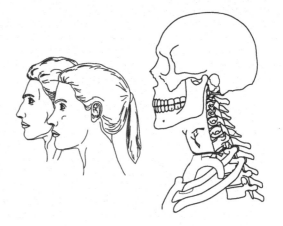

JUMBLE BrainBusters

Unscramble the Jumbles, one letter to each square, to spell words related to the human body.

#1 NJITO

#2 SUEPL

#3 OTOHT

#4 DOLOB

#5 RTAYRE

#6 CLUEMS

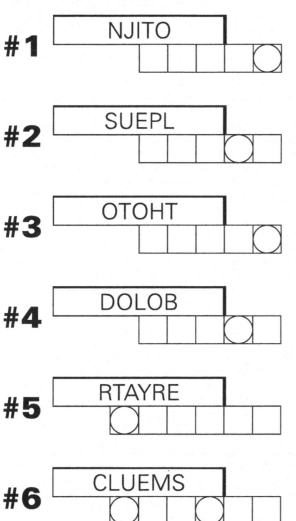

Box of Clues

Stumped? Maybe you can find a clue below. (No clue for the mystery answer.)

- Starts with *T*; ends with *H*
- Starts with *B*; ends with *D*
- Starts with *J*; ends with *T*
- Starts with *A*; ends with *Y*
- Starts with *P*; ends with *E*
- Starts with *M*; ends with *E*

Arrange the circled letters to solve the mystery answer.

MYSTERY ANSWER

MATH

JUMBLE
BrainBusters

Unscramble the Jumbled
letters, one letter to each square,
so that each equation is correct.

For example: NONTEOEOW
ONE + ONE = TWO

#1 WOEIHTOUTRFG

◯ ☐ ☐ ◯ ☐ ☐ ÷ ◯ ☐ ☐ = ☐ ☐ ☐ ☐ ◯

#2 YETEWETNNTNT

☐ ☐ ☐ ◯ ☐ ☐ ☐ − ☐ ◯ ☐ = ☐ ☐ ☐ ◯

#3 HUUOFROFRITEG

☐ ☐ ☐ ◯ + ☐ ☐ ☐ ☐ = ◯ ☐ ☐ ◯ ☐

#4 HTXIYTROTSWIYT

☐ ☐ ☐ ☐ ◯ ☐ × ☐ ☐ ☐ = ☐ ◯ ☐ ☐

#5 TEHEITEIHZGROG

☐ ☐ ☐ ☐ ☐ − ◯ ☐ ☐ ☐ ☐ = ☐ ◯ ☐ ☐

Then arrange the
circled letters to solve
the mystery equation.   **MYSTERY EQUATION**

◯◯◯◯◯ × ◯◯◯◯◯◯ = ◯◯◯◯◯

68

AROUND THE HOME

Unscramble the Jumbles, one letter to each square, to spell words related to the home.

#1 HLITG

#2 TRAYPN

#3 ESCOTL

#4 NCILIGE

#5 RZFEEER

#6 BABHTUT

Box of Clues

Stumped? Maybe you can find a clue below.

- Closet used for storing food
- Common kitchen appliance
- Pilot _____
- Room's highest part
- Plans
- Small storage room
- Wide, low vessel for water

Arrange the circled letters to solve the mystery answer.

MYSTERY ANSWER

U.S. STATE CAPITALS

Unscramble the Jumbles, one letter to each square, to spell names of U.S. state capitals.

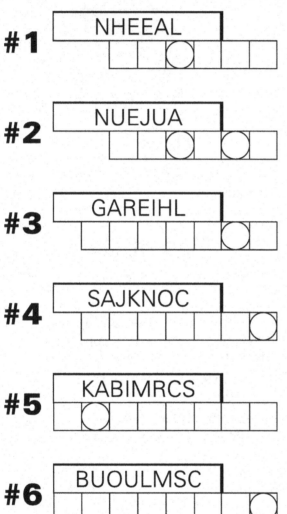

#1 NHEEAL

#2 NUEJUA

#3 GAREIHL

#4 SAJKNOC

#5 KABIMRCS

#6 BUOULMSC

Box of Clues

Stumped? Maybe you can find a clue below.

-Capital of the "Flickertail State"
-Capital of the "Buckeye State"
-Capital of the "Wolverine State"
-Capital of the "Tar Heel State"
-Capital of "Big Sky Country"
-Capital of the "Last Frontier"
-Capital of the "Magnolia State"

Arrange the circled letters to solve the mystery answer.

MYSTERY ANSWER

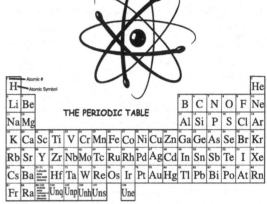

ELEMENTS

Unscramble the Jumbles, one letter to each square, to spell names of elements.

#1 ORIN

#2 DOGL

#3 NEOYGX

#4 UIELMH

#5 SDUOIM

#6 REMUCYR

Arrange the circled letters to solve the mystery answer.

THE PERIODIC TABLE

Box of Clues

Stumped? Maybe you can find a clue below. (No clue for the mystery answer.)

- Starts with *G*; ends with *D*
- Starts with *H*; ends with *M*
- Starts with *M*; ends with *Y*
- Starts with *O*; ends with *N*
- Starts with *S*; ends with *M*
- Starts with *I*; ends with *N*

MYSTERY ANSWER

CLOTHING

Unscramble the Jumbles, one letter to each square, to spell words related to clothing.

#1 NWOG

#2 FTOIUT

#3 TCJEKA

#4 OSTSRH

#5 UEDTOX

#6 ARELPAP

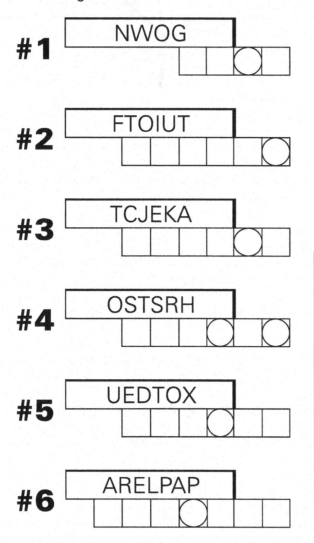

Box of Clues

Stumped? Maybe you can find a clue below.

- Starts with *S*; ends with *S*
- Starts with *T*; ends with *O*
- Starts with *O*; ends with *T*
- Starts with *G*; ends with *N*
- Starts with *S*; ends with *R*
- Starts with *A*; ends with *L*
- Starts with *J*; ends with *T*

Arrange the circled letters to solve the mystery answer.

MYSTERY ANSWER

ALL ABOUT MONEY

Unscramble the Jumbles, one letter to each square, to spell words related to money.

#1 AONL

#2 ENPNY

#3 CTKSO

#4 EIVTNS

#5 RCAEHG

#6 LBFLIODL

Box of Clues

Stumped? Maybe you can find a clue below.

-Common _____
-Borrowed money
-Commit money in an attempt to make a profit
-_____ account
-Lincoln's coin
-Wallet
-Buy now and pay later

Arrange the circled letters to solve the mystery answer.

MYSTERY ANSWER

COMPUTERS

Unscramble the Jumbles, one letter to each square, to spell words related to computers.

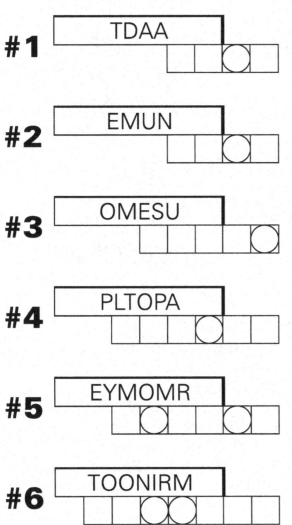

#1 TDAA

#2 EMUN

#3 OMESU

#4 PLTOPA

#5 EYMOMR

#6 TOONIRM

Box of Clues

Stumped? Maybe you can find a clue below.

-Portable computer
-Information
-Pointer controller
-Capacity for storing information
-Very large network
-Screen
-List of options in Windows

Arrange the circled letters to solve the mystery answer.

MYSTERY ANSWER

SPORTS

JUMBLE.
BrainBusters

Unscramble the Jumbles, one letter to each square, to spell words related to sports.

#1 TIMT

#2 ACHCT

#3 RTISEK

#4 SJREYE

#5 DHEDUL

#6 CHITRPE

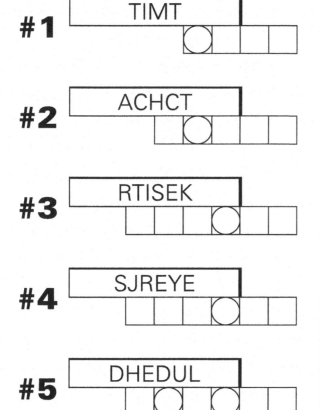

Box of Clues

Stumped? Maybe you can find a clue below. (No clue for the mystery answer.)

-Catcher's partner
-Glove
-"K"
-Play area's structure
-Meeting of the minds to discuss next play
-Outfielder objective
-Uniform top

Arrange the circled letters to solve the mystery answer.

MYSTERY ANSWER

DOUBLE JUMBLE® BRAINBUSTERS

Unscramble the Jumbles, one letter to each square, to spell words.

#1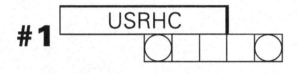
USRHC

#2
UOHGD

#3
TCIWH

#4
OWRNF

#5
RTLEIT

#6
NOTRGH

Box of Clues

Stumped? Maybe you can find a clue below. (No clues for the mystery answers.)

- Money
- Facial expression
- Infatuation
- Sorceress
- Crowd
- _____ box

Arrange the diamonded letters to solve mystery answer #1. Arrange the circled letters to solve mystery answer #2.
(The mystery answers will relate to each other.)

MYSTERY ANSWER #1

MYSTERY ANSWER #2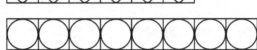

RHYMING WORDS

Unscramble the Jumbles, one letter
to each square, to spell pairs of words
that rhyme.

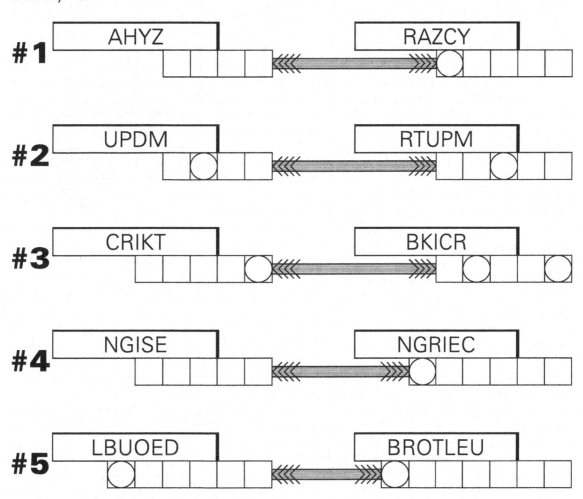

Arrange the circled letters to solve the mystery answer.
(Form two words that rhyme.)

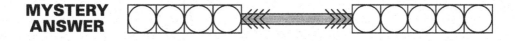

STARTS WITH A VOWEL

JUMBLE
BrainBusters

Unscramble the Jumbles, one letter to each square, to spell words that start with a vowel.

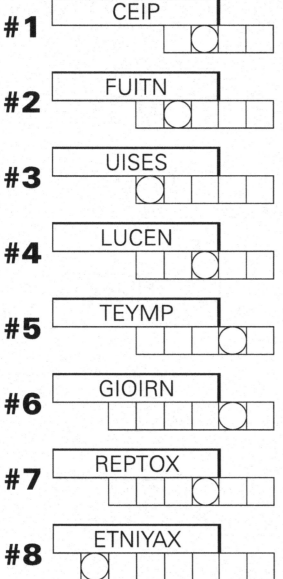

#1 CEIP

#2 FUITN

#3 UISES

#4 LUCEN

#5 TEYMP

#6 GIOIRN

#7 REPTOX

#8 ETNIYAX

Arrange the circled letters to solve the mystery answer.

Box of Clues

Stumped? Maybe you can find a clue below.

- Tension
- Void
- Type of doctor
- Send out to another country
- Matter
- Not suitable
- Male relative
- Beginning, source
- Long narrative poem

MYSTERY ANSWER

TV SHOWS

JUMBLE.
BrainBusters

Unscramble the Jumbles, one letter
to each square, to spell names of
TV shows.

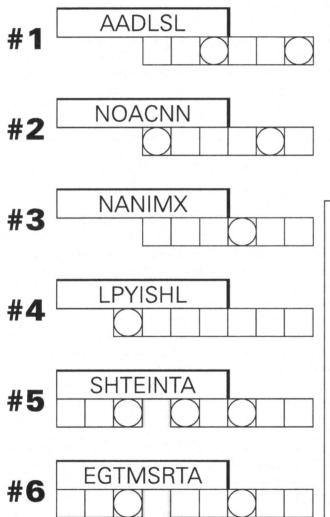

#1 AADLSL

#2 NOACNN

#3 NANIMX

#4 LPYISHL

#5 SHTEINTA

#6 EGTMSRTA

Box of Clues

Stumped? Maybe you can find a
clue below.

-1960s Roger Moore show
-Long-running CBS drama
 set in Texas
-Don Adams sitcom
-CBS detective drama starring
 William Conrad
-1960s sci-fi series featuring
 a family
-A *The Mary Tyler Moore
 Show* spin-off
-CBS detective drama starring
 Mike Connors

Arrange the circled
letters to solve the
mystery answer.

MYSTERY ANSWER

SUPER JUMBLE® CHALLENGE

JUMBLE®
BrainBusters

Unscramble the Jumbles, one letter to each square, to spell words.

#1 RFY

#2 GFLA

#3 RFOEC

#4 PULYPS

#5 MSLIEHB

#6 RNPOICEV

#7 WOUSLFERN

#8 CMIRPOCSOE

#9 ARSITGNIONE

#10 BTOUROHGREDH

Box of Clues

Stumped? Maybe you can find a clue below.

-Pedigreed animal
 -Quebec or Ontario
  -Noticeable imperfection
   -Product's public notice
    -Cook with fat
     -Air _____
      -Giving up a position
       -Demand's partner
        -_____ seed
         -Optical instrument
          -American _____

Arrange the circled letters to solve the mystery answer.

MYSTERY ANSWER

FOOD

JUMBLE BrainBusters

Unscramble the Jumbles, one letter to each square, to spell words related to food.

#1 UNIFMF

#2 RSIPHM

#3 NDUIDGP

#4 NCIKHEC

#5 OTOCUNC

#6 AELABLMT

Box of Clues

Stumped? Maybe you can find a clue below. (No clue for the mystery answer.)

-Starts with *S*; ends with *P*

-Starts with *C*; ends with *T*

-Starts with *P*; ends with *G*

-Starts with *C*; ends with *N*

-Starts with *M*; ends with *N*

-Starts with *M*; ends with *L*

Arrange the circled letters to solve the mystery answer.

MYSTERY ANSWER

PUZZLE 80

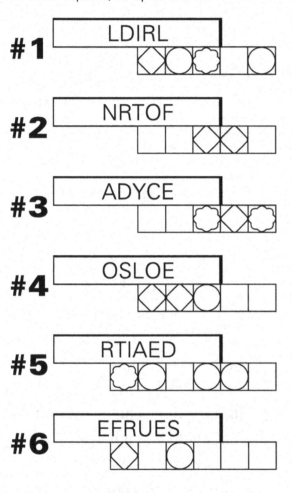

Unscramble the Jumbles, one letter to each square, to spell words.

#1 LDIRL

#2 NRTOF

#3 ADYCE

#4 OSLOE

#5 RTIAED

#6 EFRUES

JUMBLE BrainBusters

MYSTERY ANSWER #1 FISH
MYSTERY ANSWER #2 TROUT
MYSTERY ANSWER #3 UPSTRAM

MYSTERY ANSWER #1 CHEF
MYSTERY ANSWER #2 BROIL
MYSTERY ANSWER #3 SEAFOOD

Box of Clues

Stumped? Maybe you can find a clue below. (No clues for the mystery answers.)

-Cold or warm _____
-Unrestrained
-Rot
-Tongue-lashing
-Fire _____
-Garbage

Arrange the clouded letters to solve mystery answer #1. Arrange the diamonded letters to solve mystery answer #2. Arrange the circled letters to solve mystery answer #3.
(The mystery answers will relate to each other.)

MYSTERY ANSWER #1

MYSTERY ANSWER #2

MYSTERY ANSWER #3

MATH

JUMBLE
BrainBusters

Unscramble the Jumbled
letters, one letter to each square,
so that each equation is correct.

For example: NONTEOEOW
O N E + O N E = T W O

#1 ZSXSEIRIOX

☐☐☐ − ☐◯☐ = ☐◯☐☐

#2 TVFIEIVNEFE

☐☐☐☐☐ + ☐☐◯☐ = ☐☐◯

#3 HTREORNEEEETEH

☐☐☐◯☐ ÷ ☐◯☐ = ☐☐☐☐◯☐

#4 FRFIYFITZEOTFY

☐☐☐◯☐☐ − ☐☐☐☐☐☐ = ☐◯☐◯

#5 EVITWEEVSEENFVL

☐◯☐◯☐☐ − ☐☐☐☐◯ = ☐☐☐☐

Then arrange the
circled letters to solve
the mystery equation.

MYSTERY EQUATION

◯◯◯ + ◯◯◯◯ = ◯◯◯◯◯◯

U.S. STATES

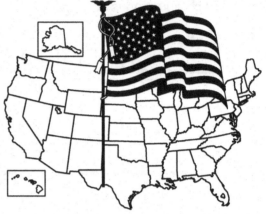

JUMBLE BrainBusters

Unscramble the Jumbles, one letter to each square, to spell names of U.S. states.

#1 RDFOIAL

#2 NZAIOAR

#3 EIGOGRA

#4 NIAVIGIR

#5 OLINISIL

#6 KAERSBAN

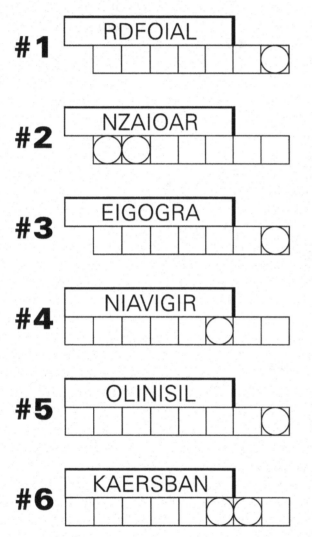

Box of Clues

Stumped? Maybe you can find a clue below.

- The last of the original 13 colonies
- South Dakota's neighbor to the south
- 25th state to enter the Union
- Home to the first permanent English settlement in America
- The "Sunshine State"
- Home to the Grand Canyon
- State on the west side of Lake Michigan

Arrange the circled letters to solve the mystery answer.

MYSTERY ANSWER

ANIMALS

Unscramble the Jumbles, one letter to each square, to spell names of animals.

#1 PIOHP

#2 BIARTB

#3 MHSIPR

#4 KEOYNM

#5 ZRGIYZL

#6 AEHNRPT

Box of Clues

Stumped? Maybe you can find a clue below.

- Starts with *S*; ends with *P*
- Starts with *R*; ends with *T*
- Starts with *T*; ends with *E*
- Starts with *G*; ends with *Y*
- Starts with *H*; ends with *O*
- Starts with *M*; ends with *Y*
- Starts with *P*; ends with *R*

Arrange the circled letters to solve the mystery answer.

MYSTERY ANSWER

DOUBLE JUMBLE® BRAINBUSTERS

Unscramble the Jumbles, one letter to each square, to spell words.

#1 RSIKM

#2 RMYEC

#3 TKENIT

#4 CTSAHW

#5 OCSMTU

#6 COCRTRE

JUMBLE BrainBusters

MYSTERY ANSWER #1 SUNNY
MYSTERY ANSWER #2 WEATHER

MYSTERY ANSWER #1 SPORTS
MYSTERY ANSWER #2 ATHLETES

MYSTERY ANSWER #1 COUNTRY
MYSTERY ANSWER #2 ETHIOPIA

Box of Clues

Stumped? Maybe you can find a clue below. (No clues for the mystery answers.)

- Long-running habit
- Young feline
- Clemency
- Type of grin
- Sample piece
- Right

Arrange the diamonded letters to solve mystery answer #1. Arrange the circled letters to solve mystery answer #2. (The mystery answers will relate to each other.)

MYSTERY ANSWER #1

MYSTERY ANSWER #2

BIRDS

JUMBLE BrainBusters

Unscramble the Jumbles, one letter to each square, to spell names of birds.

#1 EDVO

#2 BRINO

#3 EUNPING

#4 RVEUUTL

#5 ZAUZDBR

#6 ROPRWSA

Box of Clues

Stumped? Maybe you can find a clue below. (No clue for the mystery answer.)

- -Starts with *P*; ends with *N*
- **-**Starts with *D*; ends with *E*
- -Starts with *R*; ends with *N*
- **-**Starts with *B*; ends with *D*
- -Starts with *V*; ends with *E*
- **-**Starts with *S*; ends with *W*

Arrange the circled letters to solve the mystery answer.

MYSTERY ANSWER

FOOTBALL

Unscramble the Jumbles, one letter
to each square, to spell words related
to football.

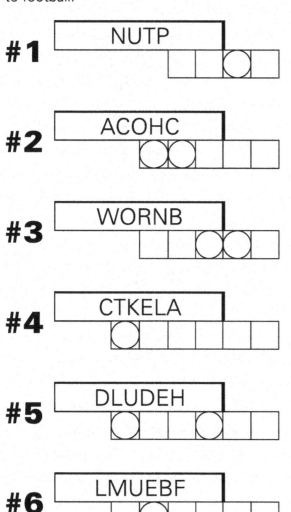

#1 NUTP

#2 ACOHC

#3 WORNB

#4 CTKELA

#5 DLUDEH

#6 LMUEBF

Box of Clues

Stumped? Maybe you can find a clue
below. (No clue for the mystery answer.)

-Cleveland Browns' Jim
-Mistake
-Short meeting
-Defensive player's goal
-Leader
-Kick

Arrange the circled letters
to solve the mystery answer.

MYSTERY ANSWER

DOUBLE JUMBLE® BRAINBUSTERS

Unscramble the Jumbles, one letter to each square, to spell words.

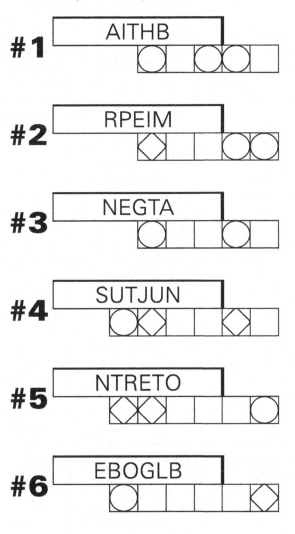

#1 AITHB

#2 RPEIM

#3 NEGTA

#4 SUTJUN

#5 NTRETO

#6 EBOGLB

JUMBLE. BrainBusters

MYSTERY ANSWER #1 SUNNY
MYSTERY ANSWER #2 WEATHER

MYSTERY ANSWER #1 SPORTS
MYSTERY ANSWER #2 ATHLETES

MYSTERY ANSWER #1 COUNTRY
MYSTERY ANSWER #2 ETHIOPIA

Box of Clues

Stumped? Maybe you can find a clue below. (No clues for the mystery answers.)

- _____ number
- _____-forming
- Bad
- Eat greedily
- Not fair
- Secret _____

Arrange the diamonded letters to solve mystery answer #1. Arrange the circled letters to solve mystery answer #2.
(The mystery answers will relate to each other.)

MYSTERY ANSWER #1

MYSTERY ANSWER #2

JUMBLE® TRIVIA

Unscramble the Jumbles, one letter
to each square, to spell words as
suggested by the trivia clues.

#1 This president's middle name
was *Simpson*.

#1 TARNG

#2 This was the first sport to be
filmed (1894).

#2 GBIONX

#3 The largest group of present-
day Mayan descendants live
in this country.

#3 VIAOLIB

#4 Brontology is the study of
this.

#4 DNHURTE

#5 Sir Isaac Pitman invented
a modern version of this time-
saving system in the mid-1800s.

#5 ARTSOHNDH

Arrange the circled letters
to solve the mystery answer. There are about 3,000 of these in New York City.

MYSTERY ANSWER ⬭⬭⬭ ⬭⬭⬭ ⬭⬭⬭⬭⬭⬭⬭

ANIMALS

Unscramble the Jumbles, one letter to each square, to spell names of animals.

#1 LAOAK

#2 TLSHO

#3 RLIADZ

#4 KAJALC

#5 TCOOEY

#6 EGHROP

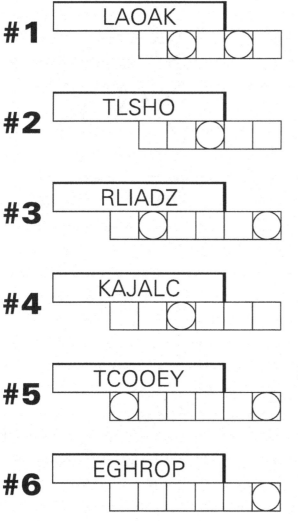

Box of Clues

Stumped? Maybe you can find a clue below. (No clue for the mystery answer.)

- Stocky rodent
- Suborder of reptile
- Wild North American dog
- Canine with large ears and a bushy tail found in Africa and Asia
- Powerful, carnivorous reptile
- Extremely slow-moving mammal
- Australian marsupial

Arrange the circled letters to solve the mystery answer.

MYSTERY ANSWER

TV SHOWS

JUMBLE BrainBusters

Unscramble the Jumbles, one letter to each square, to spell names of TV shows.

#1 STWEERB

#2 VOUSRVIR

#3 NORESNAE

#4 SIDAONUSR

#5 CMIAIMVIE

#6 SEPYTNTEM

Box of Clues

Stumped? Maybe you can find a clue below.

- ABC sitcom named after its star
- NBC police drama set in Florida
- ABC sitcom starring Emmanuel Lewis
- NBC sitcom set in south Florida
- ABC sitcom set millions of years in the past
- NBC drama that shares its name with a city
- CBS reality show

Arrange the circled letters to solve the mystery answer.

MYSTERY ANSWER

THE HUMAN BODY

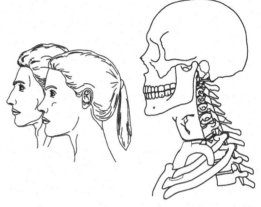

Unscramble the Jumbles, one letter to each square, to spell words related to the human body.

#1 LSUEP

#2 ANLDG

#3 LEPENS

#4 OAHRTT

#5 MNAYTOA

#6 EOKLTNSE

Box of Clues

Stumped? Maybe you can find a clue below.

-Human framework
-Adrenal _____
-Muscular tube that passes from the pharynx down the neck
-Regular throbbing
-Air and food passageway
-Highly vascular ductless organ that is located in the left abdominal region
-Structural makeup

Arrange the circled letters to solve the mystery answer.

MYSTERY ANSWER

MEANS THE OPPOSITE

JUMBLE
BrainBusters

Unscramble the Jumbles, one letter
to each square, to spell pairs of words
that have opposite or nearly opposite
meanings.

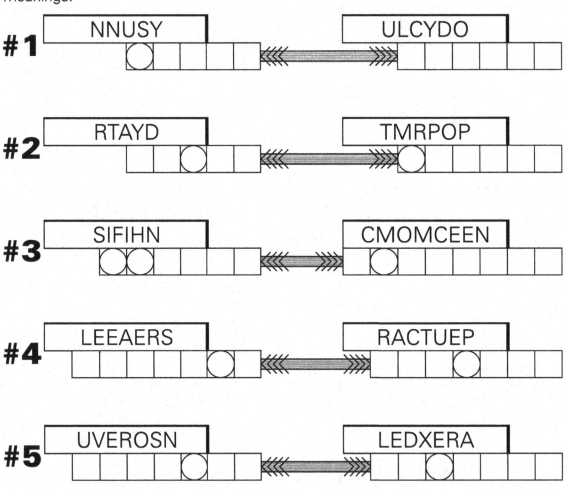

#1 NNUSY — ULCYDO

#2 RTAYD — TMRPOP

#3 SIFIHN — CMOMCEEN

#4 LEEAERS — RACTUEP

#5 UVEROSN — LEDXERA

Arrange the circled letters to solve the mystery answer.
(Form two words that have the opposite or nearly
opposite meanings.)

**MYSTERY
ANSWER**

MATH

JUMBLE
BrainBusters

Unscramble the Jumbled
letters, one letter to each square,
so that each equation is correct.

For example:

NONTEOEOW

ONE + ONE = TWO

#1 ZTNTEEORNE

$$\square\square\bigcirc\square - \square\square\square\square = \square\square\square\bigcirc$$

#2 OWZOTEORERZ

$$\square\bigcirc\square \times \square\bigcirc\square\square = \square\bigcirc\square\square$$

#3 XTELISVEISWX

$$\square\square\square\square\square\bigcirc - \square\square\square = \square\bigcirc\square\square$$

#4 NEEVONWIESTN

$$\bigcirc\square\bigcirc\square\square + \bigcirc\square\square = \square\square\square\square$$

#5 VEFILSIEEEENVX

$$\bigcirc\square\square\square\square + \square\square\square\square = \square\square\square\bigcirc\square\square$$

Then arrange the
circled letters to solve
the mystery equation.

MYSTERY EQUATION

$$\bigcirc\bigcirc\bigcirc\bigcirc\bigcirc - \bigcirc\bigcirc\bigcirc\bigcirc = \bigcirc\bigcirc\bigcirc$$

POETRY

JUMBLE BrainBusters

Unscramble the Jumbles, one letter to each square, to spell words found in the poem.

#1 LYFOL

#2 RTUHT

#3 TRUUEF

#4 RTOORWOM

#5 GIOLEDB

#6 HEBIDN

The Trickery of Time
by Kim E. Nolan

I took a lot for granted
In the _____ #1 of my youth
I thought time was boundless
But now I know the _____ #2

Always dreaming of the _____ #3
I frittered time away
I only thought about _____ #4
I never lived for my today

Time was cruel and _____ #5 me
Life happened way too fast
Now that it's _____ #6 me
My thoughts are of my past

Arrange the circled letters
to solve the mystery answer.
(The mystery answer is not
in the poem.)

MYSTERY ANSWER

AROUND THE HOME

Unscramble the Jumbles, one letter to each square, to spell words related to the home.

#1 TIPAO

#2 CPRHO

#3 NIDSIG

#4 WDIWON

#5 ONLCAYB

#6 LNBPIGUM

Arrange the circled letters to solve the mystery answer.

Interesting Home Facts

The White House and its landscaped grounds in Washington, D.C., occupy 18 acres of ground.

The White House has six floors (counting two basements), 132 rooms, 32 bathrooms, 147 windows, 412 doors, 12 chimneys, three elevators, and seven staircases.

MYSTERY ANSWER

MATH TERMS

JUMBLE. BrainBusters

Unscramble the Jumbles, one letter to each square, to spell words related to math.

#1 GIDIT

#2 TRIOA

#3 UMISN

#4 NAERWS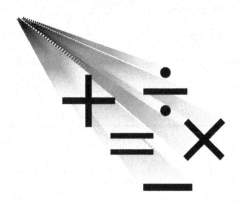

#5 CDROUTP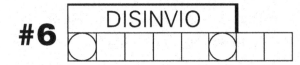

#6 DISINVIO

Box of Clues

Stumped? Maybe you can find a clue below.

-Proportion
-Solution
-Number resulting from the multiplication of two or more numbers
-Long _____
-Double-_____
-_____ sign
-Operation of combining numbers

Arrange the circled letters to solve the mystery answer.

MYSTERY ANSWER

STARTS WITH A VOWEL

Unscramble the Jumbles, one letter to each square, to spell words that start with a vowel.

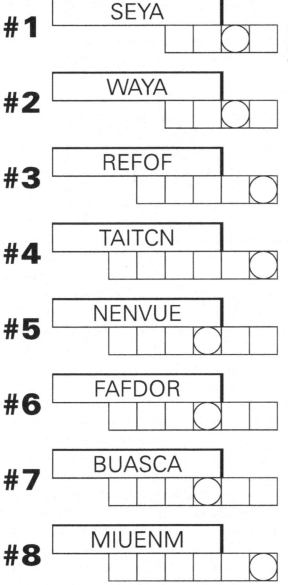

#1 SEYA

#2 WAYA

#3 REFOF

#4 TAITCN

#5 NENVUE

#6 FAFDOR

#7 BUASCA

#8 MIUENM

Box of Clues

Stumped? Maybe you can find a clue below.

- Be capable of paying for
- Absent from a place
- Unaffected
- Simple
- Price named by one proposing to buy
- Unequal
- Cloudy
- Early counter
- Together

Arrange the circled letters to solve the mystery answer.

MYSTERY ANSWER

ALL ABOUT MONEY

JUMBLE
BrainBusters

Unscramble the Jumbles, one letter to each square, to spell words related to money.

#1 ECCKH

#2 LAEWTL

#3 RIPEETC

#4 ACIFNEN

#5 NCOIGSL

#6 ENURCYCR

Box of Clues

Stumped? Maybe you can find a clue below. (No clue for the mystery answer.)

-Meeting of parties to a real-estate deal
-Blank _____
-Billfold
-Transaction's written record
-Coins, treasury notes, and banknotes
-_____ company or charge

Arrange the circled letters to solve the mystery answer.

MYSTERY ANSWER

SUPER JUMBLE® CHALLENGE

Unscramble the Jumbles, one letter to each square, to spell words.

JUMBLE BrainBusters

#1 GYU

#2 LAFH

#3 NLAPK

#4 NFSIOU

#5 LTSUTEH

#6 AGMOTGER

#7 PASADPERN

#8 ABEOHRENDF

#9 DECERELAERH

#10 STAINSIMSONR

Box of Clues

Stumped? Maybe you can find a clue below.

-Heavy, thick board
-Abrasive smoothing material
-Causing intense sorrow
-Sun's source of power
-Spirited team supporter
-Automatic _____
-Fifty percent
-Previously
-Home loan
-Man
-Space _____

Arrange the circled letters to solve the mystery answer.

MYSTERY ANSWER

STARTS WITH M

Unscramble the Jumbles, one letter to each square, to spell words that start with M.

JUMBLE BrainBusters

#1 GLINEM

#2 TOMHDE

#3 NEMMTO

#4 NACMIEH

#5 BOMILXA

#6 SEMYRYT

#7 RUSEAEM

#8 GAENARM

MMMMMM
MMMMMM
MMMMMM
MMMMM

Box of Clues

Stumped? Maybe you can find a clue below.

-Head coach in baseball
-Letter container
-Ascertain the extent of
-Mix
-_____ payment
-Instant
-Washing _____
-Enigma, puzzle
-Systematic procedure

Arrange the circled letters to solve the mystery answer.

MYSTERY ANSWER

WARS AND THE MILITARY

Unscramble the Jumbles, one letter
to each square, to spell words related
to wars and the military.

#1 TATEYR

#2 CETEFD

#3 TVRIEAP

#4 RAMILDA

#5 FWREARA

#6 ONAISINV

Box of Clues

Stumped? Maybe you can find a clue
below.

-Starts with *W*; ends with *E*
-Starts with *A*; ends with *L*
-Starts with *D*; ends with *T*
-Starts with *T*; ends with *Y*
-Starts with *V*; ends with *S*
-Starts with *P*; ends with *E*
-Starts with *I*; ends with *N*

Arrange the circled letters
to solve the mystery answer.

MYSTERY ANSWER

ADJECTIVES

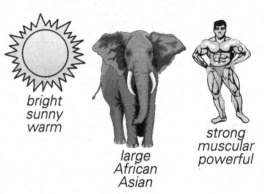

JUMBLE BrainBusters

Unscramble the Jumbles, one letter to each square, to spell adjectives.

#1 SOIYN

#2 AMLYN

#3 CVIUSIO

#4 NISTEEN

#5 DFINEYRL

#6 OAINNRTG

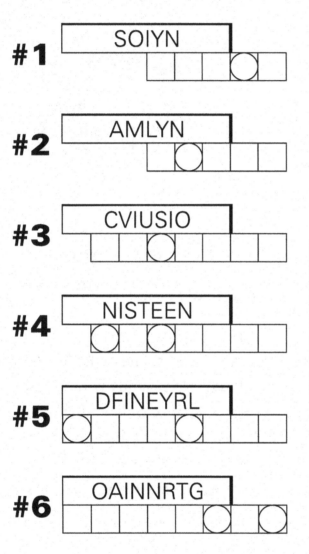

bright
sunny
warm

large
African
Asian

strong
muscular
powerful

Box of Clues

Stumped? Maybe you can find a clue below.

-Masculine, macho
-Amicable, neighborly
-Loud
-Stupendous, tremendous
-Oblivious
-Bad, evil, immoral, sinful, wicked
-Concentrated

Arrange the circled letters to solve the mystery answer.

MYSTERY ANSWER

U.S. PRESIDENTS

Unscramble the Jumbles, one letter to each square, to spell the last names of U.S. presidents.

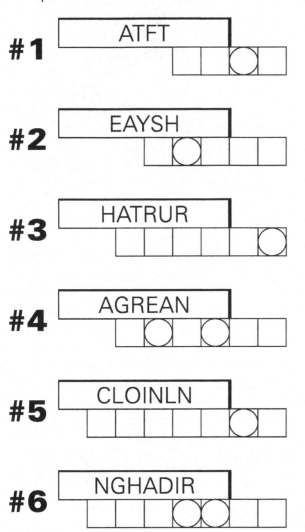

#1 ATFT

#2 EAYSH

#3 HATRUR

#4 AGREAN

#5 CLOINLN

#6 NGHADIR

Arrange the circled letters to solve the mystery answer.

Box of Clues

Stumped? Maybe you can find a clue below.

-Rutherford B. _____
-President that shared his last name with the capital of Nebraska
-President who had the same name as a present-day comic strip character
-Warren G. _____
-27th U.S. president
-President who had the same last name as a popular Dudley Moore movie
-40th U.S. president

MYSTERY ANSWER

JUMBLE BrainBusters

MOVIES

Unscramble the Jumbles, one letter to each square, to spell names of movies.

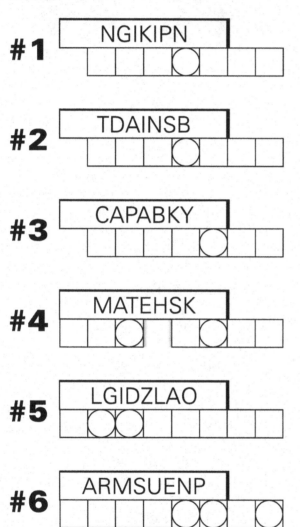

#1 NGIKIPN

#2 TDAINSB

#3 CAPABKY

#4 MATEHSK

#5 LGIDZLAO

#6 ARMSUENP

Arrange the circled letters to solve the mystery answer.

Box of Clues

Stumped? Maybe you can find a clue below.

-2001 Bruce Willis, Billy Bob Thornton movie
-1998 sci-fi movie
-1978 movie about a superhero
-1996 comedy about a bowler
-1998 monster movie
-1994 Jim Carrey comedy
-1999 Mel Gibson movie

MYSTERY ANSWER

OUTER SPACE

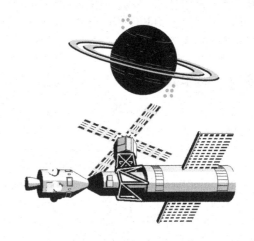

Unscramble the Jumbles, one letter to each square, to spell words related to outer space.

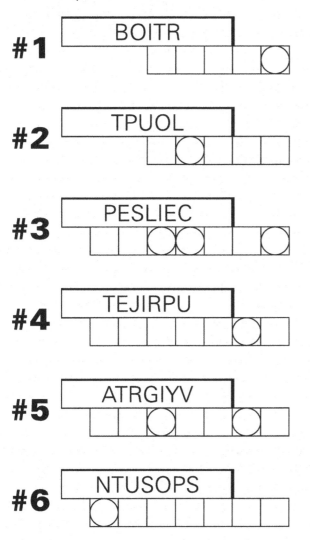

#1 BOITR

#2 TPUOL

#3 PESLIEC

#4 TEJIRPU

#5 ATRGIYV

#6 NTUSOPS

Box of Clues

Stumped? Maybe you can find a clue below.

- Largest planet in our solar system
- Lunar or solar _____
- Moon's designation in relation to the planet it encircles
- Important universal force
- Moon path
- Smallest planet in our solar system
- Disturbance on the outermost part of a star

Arrange the circled letters to solve the mystery answer.

MYSTERY ANSWER

MATH

JUMBLE BrainBusters

Unscramble the Jumbled
letters, one letter to each square,
so that each equation is correct.

For example: NONTEOEOW
ONE + ONE = TWO

#1 OEEONNOEN

◯□□ × ◯□□ = □□□

#2 WFROTOTOUW

□□□◯ ÷ □◯□ = □◯□

#3 TSEIHREEINNX

□◯□ + ◯◯□□□□ = □□□□

#4 RWFOTOEHTGIU

◯□◯□ × ◯□□ = □□◯□□◯

#5 ZSVNSNEEEVROEE

□□□□□□ − □□□◯□ = □□□□◯

Then arrange the
circled letters to solve
the mystery equation.

MYSTERY EQUATION

◯◯◯ + ◯◯◯ = ◯◯◯◯◯ − ◯◯◯◯

COUNTRIES

JUMBLE
BrainBusters

Unscramble the Jumbles, one letter to each square, to spell names of countries.

#1 LIAYT

#2 NKYAE

#3 DAIELNC

#4 PIOEHIAT

#5 NTAIHDAL

#6 BOMLAOIC

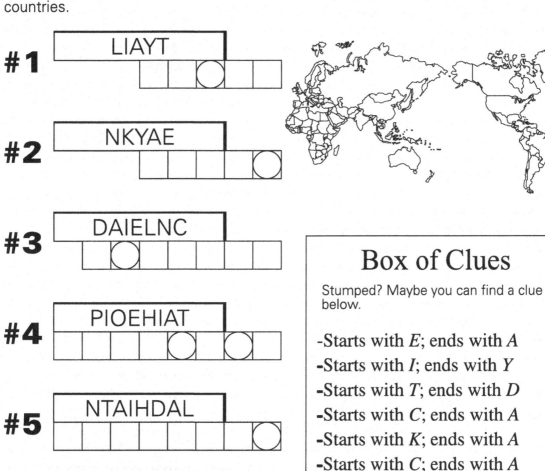

Box of Clues

Stumped? Maybe you can find a clue below.

- Starts with *E*; ends with *A*
- Starts with *I*; ends with *Y*
- Starts with *T*; ends with *D*
- Starts with *C*; ends with *A*
- Starts with *K*; ends with *A*
- Starts with *C*; ends with *A*
- Starts with *I*; ends with *D*

Arrange the circled letters to solve the mystery answer.

MYSTERY ANSWER

OCCUPATIONS

JUMBLE BrainBusters

Unscramble the Jumbles, one letter to each square, to spell names of occupations.

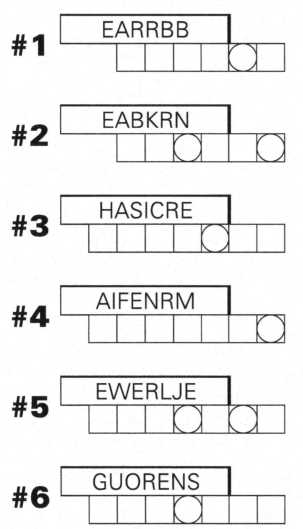

#1 EARRBB

#2 EABKRN

#3 HASICRE

#4 AIFENRM

#5 EWERLJE

#6 GUORENS

Box of Clues

Stumped? Maybe you can find a clue below. (No clue for the mystery answer.)

- Starts with *S*; ends with *N*
- Starts with *B*; ends with *R*
- Starts with *F*; ends with *N*
- Starts with *C*; ends with *R*
- Starts with *J*; ends with *R*
- Starts with *B*; ends with *R*

Arrange the circled letters to solve the mystery answer.

MYSTERY ANSWER

ALL ABOUT MUSIC

Unscramble the Jumbles, one letter to each square, to spell words related to music.

#1 RHAP ◯

#2 SOGN ◯

#3 BLMAU ◯

#4 ZOMRAT ◯◯

#5 DELYMO ◯ ◯

#6 RECOCNT ◯ ◯

Box of Clues

Stumped? Maybe you can find a clue below.

- Starts with *M*; ends with *Y*
- Starts with *C*; ends with *T*
- Starts with *M*; ends with *T*
- Starts with *A*; ends with *M*
- Starts with *H*; ends with *P*
- Starts with *O*; ends with *A*
- Starts with *S*; ends with *G*

Arrange the circled letters to solve the mystery answer.

MYSTERY ANSWER

◯◯◯◯◯◯◯◯◯◯

U.S. STATE CAPITALS

Unscramble the Jumbles, one letter to each square, to spell names of U.S. state capitals.

#1 RRIEEP

#2 EOTPAK

#3 NSTOOB

#4 LMOYIAP

#5 ROCCDON

#6 UOHOULNL

Box of Clues

Stumped? Maybe you can find a clue below.

- Capital of the southernmost state
- Capital of the most populous state in New England
- Capital of Kansas
- Capital of the "Chinook State"
- Capital of the "Old Line State"
- Capital of New Hampshire
- Capital of South Dakota

Arrange the circled letters to solve the mystery answer.

MYSTERY ANSWER

MEANS THE SAME

JUMBLE BrainBusters

Unscramble the Jumbles, one letter to each square, to spell pairs of words that have the same or similar meanings.

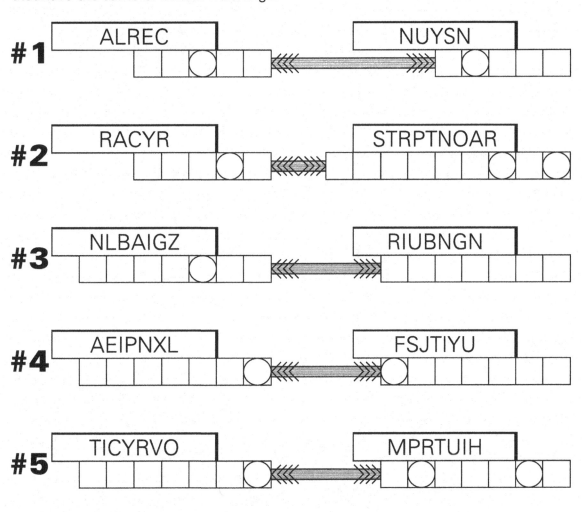

#1 ALREC — NUYSN

#2 RACYR — STRPTNOAR

#3 NLBAIGZ — RIUBNGN

#4 AEIPNXL — FSJTIYU

#5 TICYRVO — MPRTUIH

Arrange the circled letters to solve the mystery answer.
(Form two words that have the same or similar meanings.)

MYSTERY ANSWER

TRIPLE JUMBLE® BRAINBUSTERS

JUMBLE BrainBusters

Unscramble the Jumbles, one letter to each square, to spell words.

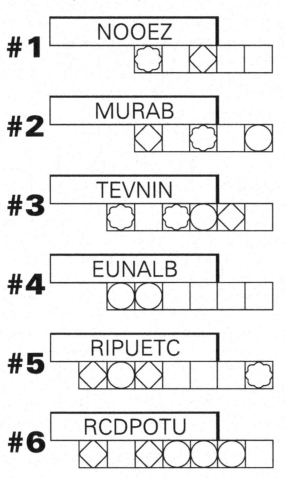

#1 NOOEZ

#2 MURAB

#3 TEVNIN

#4 EUNALB

#5 RIPUETC

#6 RCDPOTU

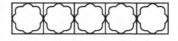
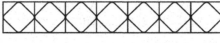

MYSTERY ANSWER #1 FISH
MYSTERY ANSWER #2 TROUT
MYSTERY ANSWER #3 UPSTRAM

MYSTERY ANSWER #1 CHEF
MYSTERY ANSWER #2 BROIL
MYSTERY ANSWER #3 SEAFOOD

Box of Clues

Stumped? Maybe you can find a clue below. (No clues for the mystery answers.)

-Create
-_____ layer
-Space cloud
-Cuban dance
-By-_____
-_____ window

Arrange the clouded letters to solve mystery answer #1. Arrange the diamonded letters to solve mystery answer #2. Arrange the circled letters to solve mystery answer #3.
(The mystery answers will relate to each other.)

MYSTERY ANSWER #1

MYSTERY ANSWER #2

MYSTERY ANSWER #3

AUTOMOBILES

JUMBLE
BrainBusters

Unscramble the Jumbles, one letter to each square, to spell words related to automobiles.

#1 NURKT

#2 ARIOD

#3 OCEPU

#4 KIUCPP

#5 FATFCIR

#6 SOINWDW

Interesting Automotive Facts

United States courts devote about half their time to cases involving automobiles.

A car uses about 1.5 ounces of gas idling for one minute.

The initials *M.G.* on the British-made automobile stand for "Morris Garage."

Arrange the circled letters to solve the mystery answer.

MYSTERY ANSWER

SPORTS

JUMBLE®
BrainBusters

Unscramble the Jumbles, one letter
to each square, to spell words related
to sports.

#1 LGOEV

#2 ENTSIN

#3 KOIERO

#4 UEOLBD

#5 RWFAYIA

#6 NMIODAD

Box of Clues

Stumped? Maybe you can find a clue
below. (No clue for the mystery answer.)

-Connors' sport
-Bases' shape
-Baseball hit
-Mitt
-First-year player
-Driver's landing area

Arrange the circled letters
to solve the mystery answer.

MYSTERY ANSWER

ENDS IN Y

Unscramble the Jumbles, one letter to each square, to spell words that end in Y.

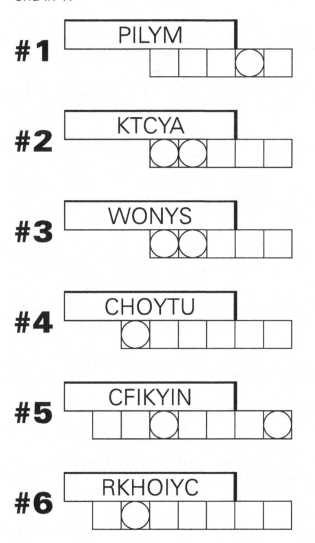

#1 PILYM

#2 KTCYA

#3 WONYS

#4 CHOYTU

#5 CFIKYIN

#6 RKHOIYC

Box of Clues

Stumped? Maybe you can find a clue below.

-Sensitive
-Fussy
-Gaudy
-North American hardwood
-Without delay
-Wintry
-Infer

Arrange the circled letters to solve the mystery answer.

MYSTERY ANSWER

ELEMENTS

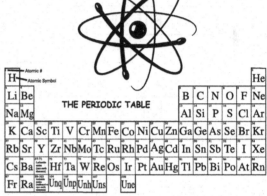

Unscramble the Jumbles, one letter to each square, to spell names of elements.

#1 DIOIEN

#2 PECPRO

#3 OISICNL

#4 UCLCMIA

#5 RNTIENGO

#6 NUAUMIML

THE PERIODIC TABLE

Box of Clues

Stumped? Maybe you can find a clue below. (No clue for the mystery answer.)

- Starts with *A*; ends with *M*
- Starts with *I*; ends with *E*
- Starts with *N*; ends with *N*
- Starts with *S*; ends with *N*
- Starts with *C*; ends with *R*
- Starts with *C*; ends with *M*

Arrange the circled letters to solve the mystery answer.

MYSTERY ANSWER

COMPUTERS

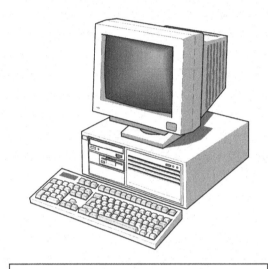

Unscramble the Jumbles, one letter to each square, to spell words related to computers.

#1 TYEB

#2 CLKIC

#3 LDEEET

#4 PLOYPF

#5 AORFTM

#6 DWNIOSW

Box of Clues

Stumped? Maybe you can find a clue below. (No clue for the mystery answer.)

-Double-_____
-Arrange stored data in a particular configuration
-_____ disk
-Group of binary digits processed as a unit
-Erase
-B.G.'s program

Arrange the circled letters to solve the mystery answer.

MYSTERY ANSWER

WEATHER

JUMBLE BrainBusters

Unscramble the Jumbles, one letter to each square, to spell words related to weather.

#1 LIDM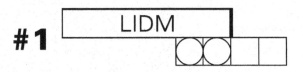

#2 DOLOF

#3 UDLOYC

#4 STIRTWE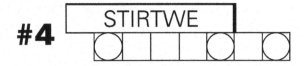

#5 LAFLRIAN

#6 SRERUEPS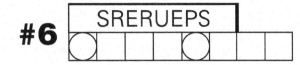

Box of Clues

Stumped? Maybe you can find a clue below.

- Tornado
- Warm
- Deluge
- Large disturbance that forms over water
- Measured liquid precipitation
- Mostly _____
- What a barometer measures

Arrange the circled letters to solve the mystery answer.

MYSTERY ANSWER

DOUBLE JUMBLE BRAINBUSTERS

Unscramble the Jumbles, one letter to each square, to spell words.

#1 ABSRS

#2 TNOHC

#3 SOUFIN

#4 TLREET

#5 XEDELU

#6 PAIGEM

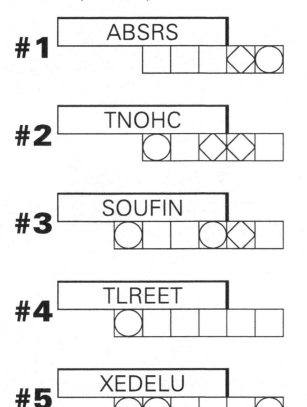

JUMBLE BrainBusters

MYSTERY ANSWER #1 SUNNY
MYSTERY ANSWER #2 WEATHER

MYSTERY ANSWER #1 SPORTS
MYSTERY ANSWER #2 ATHLETES

MYSTERY ANSWER #1 COUNTRY
MYSTERY ANSWER #2 ETHIOPIA

Box of Clues

Stumped? Maybe you can find a clue below. (No clues for the mystery answers.)

-Luxurious, sumptuous
-Jay relative
-_____ brand
-Chain _____
-Sun's power source
-Top-_____

Arrange the diamonded letters to solve mystery answer #1. Arrange the circled letters to solve mystery answer #2.
(The mystery answers will relate to each other.)

MYSTERY ANSWER #1

MYSTERY ANSWER #2

CLOTHING

Unscramble the Jumbles, one letter
to each square, to spell words related
to clothing.

#1 RPAAK

#2 ARCFS

#3 BAIFRC

#4 USLEBO

#5 MEURJP

#6 ANSKREE

Arrange the circled letters
to solve the mystery answer.

Box of Clues

Stumped? Maybe you can find a clue
below. (No clue for the mystery answer.)

-Starts with *B*; ends with *E*
-Starts with *S*; ends with *F*
-Starts with *J*; ends with *R*
-Starts with *F*; ends with *C*
-Starts with *P*; ends with *A*
-Starts with *S*; ends with *R*

MYSTERY ANSWER

JUMBLE®

BrainBusters

ADVANCED
PUZZLES

FOOD

JUMBLE
BrainBusters

Unscramble the Jumbles, one letter
to each square, to spell words related
to food.

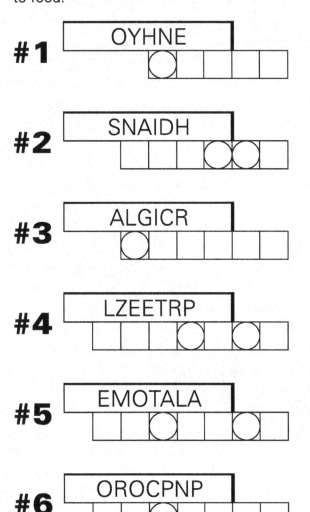

#1 OYHNE

#2 SNAIDH

#3 ALGICR

#4 LZEETRP

#5 EMOTALA

#6 OROCPNP

Box of Clues

Stumped? Maybe you can find a clue
below.

-Buttered _____
-Type of porridge
-Type of pastry
-Salted _____
-Pasta dish
-Sweet product
-_____ salt

Arrange the circled letters
to solve the mystery answer.

MYSTERY ANSWER

TRIPLE JUMBLE® BRAINBUSTERS

JUMBLE BrainBusters

Unscramble the Jumbles, one letter to each square, to spell words.

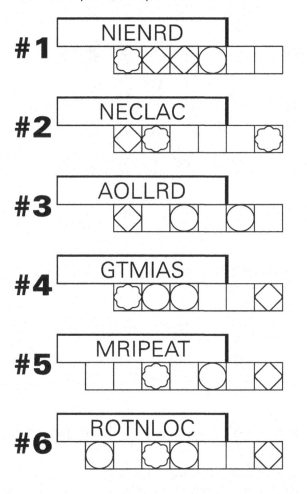

#1 NIENRD

#2 NECLAC

#3 AOLLRD

#4 GTMIAS

#5 MRIPEAT

#6 ROTNLOC

MYSTERY ANSWER #1 FISH
MYSTERY ANSWER #2 TROUT
MYSTERY ANSWER #3 UPSTRAM

MYSTERY ANSWER #1 CHEF
MYSTERY ANSWER #2 BROIL
MYSTERY ANSWER #3 SEAFOOD

Box of Clues

Stumped? Maybe you can find a clue below. (No clues for the mystery answers.)

-Sand _____
-Human's mammal order
-Annul
-_____ theater
-Mark of shame
-_____ tower

Arrange the clouded letters to solve mystery answer #1. Arrange the diamonded letters to solve mystery answer #2. Arrange the circled letters to solve mystery answer #3.
(The mystery answers will relate to each other.)

MYSTERY ANSWER #1

MYSTERY ANSWER #2

MYSTERY ANSWER #3

STARTS WITH R

JUMBLE BrainBusters

Unscramble the Jumbles, one letter to each square, to spell words that start with R.

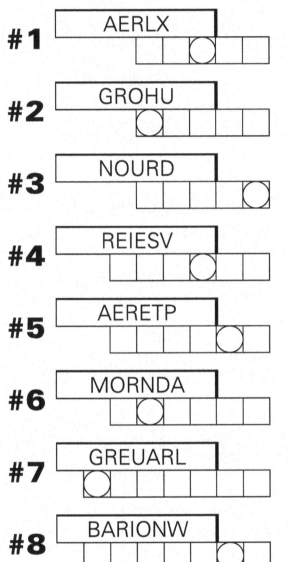

#1 AERLX

#2 GROHU

#3 NOURD

#4 REIESV

#5 AERETP

#6 MORNDA

#7 GREUARL

#8 BARIONW

R R R R R R
R R R R R R
R R R R R R
R R R R R R

Box of Clues

Stumped? Maybe you can find a clue below.

-Harsh
-Haphazard
-Circle's adjective
-Routine, normal
-Change
-_____ tracks
-Colorful weather phenomenon
-Rerun
-Take it easy

Arrange the circled letters to solve the mystery answer.

MYSTERY ANSWER

MATH

JUMBLE
BrainBusters

Unscramble the Jumbled
letters, one letter to each square,
so that each equation is correct.

For example: NONTEOEOW
O N E + O N E = T W O

#1 VFIFIONEEVE

◯ ☐ ☐ ☐ ÷ ☐ ☐ ◯ ☐ = ◯ ☐ ☐

#2 EVSVNFIEWOTE

☐ ☐ ☐ ☐ ◯ − ☐ ☐ ☐ ◯ = ☐ ☐ ☐

#3 GORUFOFRUEITH

☐ ☐ ☐ ◯ + ☐ ☐ ☐ ☐ ☐ = ◯ ☐ ☐ ☐ ☐ ☐

#4 EEITEGTOSIWTNHX

☐ ◯ ☐ ☐ ☐ ☐ × ☐ ☐ ◯ = ☐ ☐ ☐ ☐ ◯ ◯

#5 TETWNYRTHIYNTET

☐ ◯ ☐ + ◯ ☐ ☐ ◯ ☐ ☐ = ☐ ◯ ☐ ☐ ☐ ☐

Then arrange the
circled letters to solve
the mystery equation.

MYSTERY EQUATION

◯◯◯ + ◯◯◯ = ◯◯◯◯◯ − ◯◯◯◯◯

WARS AND THE MILITARY

JUMBLE
BrainBusters

Unscramble the Jumbles, one letter to each square, to spell words related to wars and the military.

#1 METLEH

#2 PWANOE

#3 TOOPILC

#4 AOUGBTN

#5 ALKODEBC

#6 REARILTYL

Box of Clues

Stumped? Maybe you can find a clue below.

-Armed ship of shallow draft
-Chemical _____
-Weapons
-a U.S. military decoration
-Aircraft's second in command
-Isolation by a warring nation of an enemy area by troops or warships
-Head protector

Arrange the circled letters to solve the mystery answer.

MYSTERY ANSWER

TRIPLE JUMBLE® BRAINBUSTERS

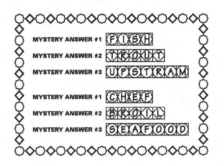

Unscramble the Jumbles, one letter to each square, to spell words.

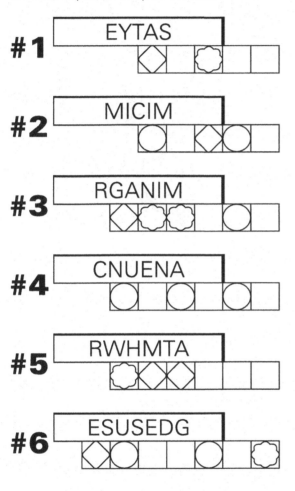

#1 EYTAS

#2 MICIM

#3 RGANIM

#4 CNUENA

#5 RWHMTA

#6 ESUSEDG

MYSTERY ANSWER #1 FISH
MYSTERY ANSWER #2 TROUT
MYSTERY ANSWER #3 UPSTRAM

MYSTERY ANSWER #1 CHEF
MYSTERY ANSWER #2 BROIL
MYSTERY ANSWER #3 SEAFOOD

Box of Clues

Stumped? Maybe you can find a clue below. (No clues for the mystery answers.)

- Imitate
- Spare amount
- Approximated
- Fungus cells
- Heat
- Subtle quality

Arrange the clouded letters to solve mystery answer #1. Arrange the diamonded letters to solve mystery answer #2. Arrange the circled letters to solve mystery answer #3.

(The mystery answers will relate to each other.)

MYSTERY ANSWER #1

MYSTERY ANSWER #2

MYSTERY ANSWER #3

STARTS WITH A VOWEL

JUMBLE
BrainBusters

Unscramble the Jumbles, one letter to each square, to spell words that start with a vowel.

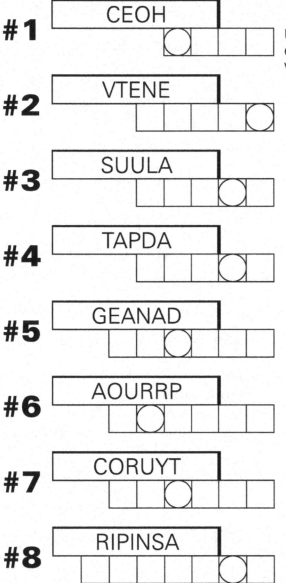

#1 CEOH

#2 VTENE

#3 SUULA

#4 TAPDA

#5 GEANAD

#6 AOURRP

#7 CORUYT

#8 RIPINSA

Box of Clues

Stumped? Maybe you can find a clue below.

- Pain reliever
- Occurrence
- Repeating sound
- Normal, routine
- Alter to fit
- Plan
- Commotion
- Instinctive desire
- Clamor

Arrange the circled letters to solve the mystery answer.

MYSTERY ANSWER

JUMBLE TRIVIA

Unscramble the Jumbles, one letter
to each square, to spell words as
suggested by the trivia clues.

#1 The first _____ was built in
London, England, in the 1860s.

#1 AWUSYB

#2 The first _____ machines in
the United States were installed
on New York City train platforms
in 1888.

#2 NVIGEND

#3 This country doesn't have any
freshwater lakes or rivers.

#3 AUEBDMR

#4 The _____ was invented in
1869 by Jonathan Scobie, an
American living in Yokohama,
Japan.

#4 SAIWKHRC

#5 The number one pizza topping
in this country is eggs.

#5 LAUARIATS

Arrange the circled letters
to solve the mystery answer.

This man secured a patent in 1873
for a self-pasting scrapbook.

MYSTERY ANSWER ⬡⬡⬡⬡⬡ ⬡⬡⬡⬡⬡

MOVIES

JUMBLE BrainBusters

Unscramble the Jumbles, one letter to each square, to spell names of movies.

#1 HRTEIMF

#2 TSEHAKM

#3 ASFARCEC

#4 MTEUMHMY

#5 AERBEHRVTA

#6 EGODAFLLSO

Box of Clues

Stumped? Maybe you can find a clue below.

- 1990 Robert De Niro drama
- 1984 comedy set in N.Y.C.
- 1993 Tom Cruise drama
- 1995 Mel Gibson drama
- 1999 Brendan Fraser adventure movie
- 1994 Jim Carrey comedy
- 1983 Al Pacino drama

Arrange the circled letters to solve the mystery answer.

MYSTERY ANSWER

SUPER JUMBLE® CHALLENGE

JUMBLE® BrainBusters

Unscramble the Jumbles, one letter to each square, to spell words.

#1 GEG

#2 LEWL

#3 ALWOL

#4 CERETJ

#5 BICEGER

#6 CBOCLOIR

#7 CHOORSOEP

#8 ATBSEBLKLA

#9 TPIULIAOCNB

#10 CEENCLOIPDAY

Box of Clues

Stumped? Maybe you can find a clue below.

-Comprehensive collection of knowledge
-Astrological forecast
-Dry or artesian _____
-Jordan or Bird's sport
-Heavenly configuration
-Refuse to accept
-_____ roll or timer
-Cabbage relative
-_____ lettuce
-Magazine or book
-Permit

Arrange the circled letters to solve the mystery answer.

MYSTERY ANSWER

PUZZLE 131

U.S. STATES

JUMBLE BrainBusters

Unscramble the Jumbles, one letter to each square, to spell names of U.S. states.

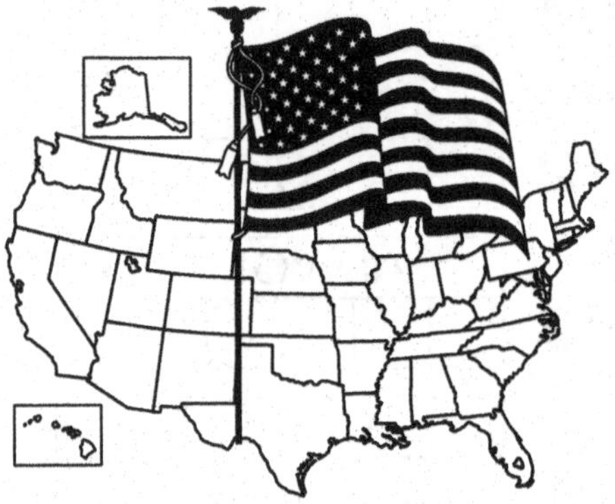

#1 AGICINHM

#2 RADEAELW

#3 ALOISINAU

#4 NIWIOCSNS

#5 STNEEESNE

#6 FRICLIOANA

★JUMBLE® Trivia Quick Quiz

What state is nicknamed the "Green Mountain State"?

TEOVRNM

ANSWER:

Arrange the circled letters to solve the mystery answer.

MYSTERY ANSWER

U.S. PRESIDENTS

Unscramble the Jumbles, one letter
to each square, to spell the last names of
U.S. presidents.

#1 ETLRY

#2 LOAYRT

#3 VHOREO

#4 TCNINOL

#5 RSARINHO

#6 OGDOIECL

Arrange the circled letters
to solve the mystery answer.

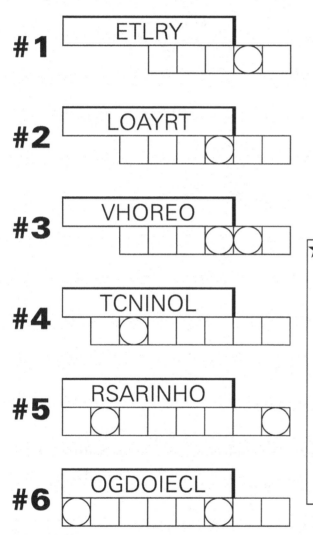

★ **JUMBLE® Trivia** Quick Quiz

Which U.S. president was
the first president to live
in the White House (then
called the Executive
Mansion)?

MANAODJSH

ANSWER:

MYSTERY ANSWER

OCCUPATIONS

Unscramble the Jumbles, one letter to each square, to spell names of occupations.

#1 LPTIO

#2 LEURBT

#3 LEAORTR

#4 SUIAMNIC

#5 NHEACICM

#6 CTCOUNORD

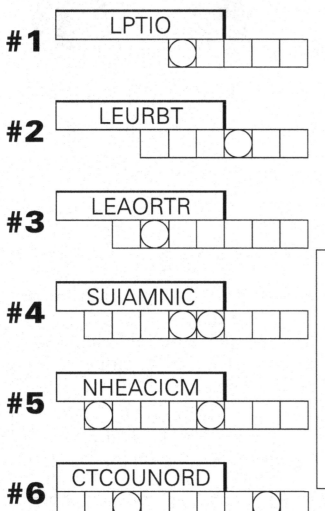

Box of Clues

Stumped? Maybe you can find a clue below. (No clue for the mystery answer.)

- Starts with *R*; ends with *R*
- Starts with *P*; ends with *T*
- Starts with *C*; ends with *R*
- Starts with *B*; ends with *R*
- Starts with *M*; ends with *N*
- Starts with *M*; ends with *C*

Arrange the circled letters to solve the mystery answer.

MYSTERY ANSWER

ALL ABOUT MUSIC

Unscramble the Jumbles, one letter to each square, to spell words related to music.

#1 LOAKP

#2 AIUGRT

#3 AOSTAN

#4 OLICOPC

#5 ABOSNOS

#6 NMIAOLND

Arrange the circled letters to solve the mystery answer.

Box of Clues

Stumped? Maybe you can find a clue below.

-Steel _____
-Shrill flute
-Instrumental musical composition typically of three or four movements in contrasting forms and keys
-_____ music
-Lively style of dance music
-Musical instrument of the lute family that usually has a pear-shaped body and a fretted neck
-Double-reed woodwind

MYSTERY ANSWER

EUROPEAN COUNTRIES

Unscramble the Jumbles, one letter to each square, to spell names of European countries.

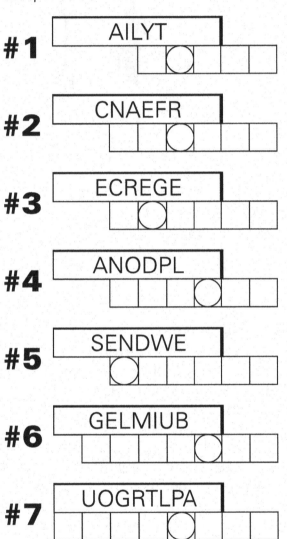

#1 AILYT

#2 CNAEFR

#3 ECREGE

#4 ANODPL

#5 SENDWE

#6 GELMIUB

#7 UOGRTLPA

Arrange the circled letters to solve the mystery answer.

Box of Clues

Stumped? Maybe you can find a clue below.

-Switzerland's southern neighbor
-Slovenia's northern neighbor
-Home to Brussels
-Home to Lisbon
-Home to Paris
-Norway's eastern neighbor
-Home to Warsaw
-Home to Athens

MYSTERY ANSWER

TRIPLE JUMBLE® BRAINBUSTERS

Unscramble the Jumbles, one letter to each square, to spell words.

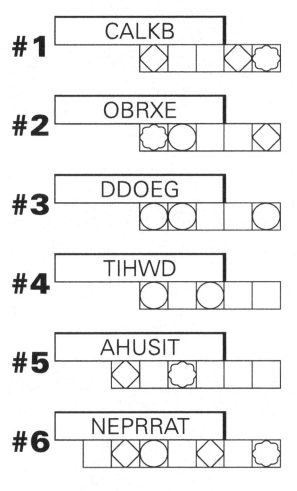

#1 CALKB

#2 OBRXE

#3 DDOEG

#4 TIHWD

#5 AHUSIT

#6 NEPRRAT

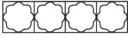
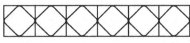

JUMBLE BrainBusters

MYSTERY ANSWER #1 FISH
MYSTERY ANSWER #2 TROUT
MYSTERY ANSWER #3 UPSTREAM

MYSTERY ANSWER #1 CHEF
MYSTERY ANSWER #2 BROIL
MYSTERY ANSWER #3 SEAFOOD

Box of Clues

Stumped? Maybe you can find a clue below. (No clues for the mystery answers.)

-Elude
-_____ belt
-Horizontal measurement
-Fighter
-Break
-Silent _____

Arrange the clouded letters to solve mystery answer #1. Arrange the diamonded letters to solve mystery answer #2. Arrange the circled letters to solve mystery answer #3.
(The mystery answers will relate to each other.)

MYSTERY ANSWER #1

MYSTERY ANSWER #2

MYSTERY ANSWER #3

MATH TERMS

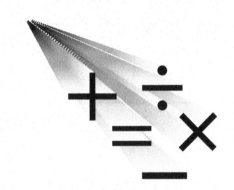

Unscramble the Jumbles, one letter
to each square, to spell words related
to math.

#1 CFOTRA

#2 MEURBN

#3 RAGLEAB
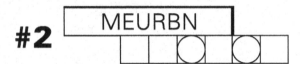

#4 LOFUAMR

#5 NFITIYIN

#6 TOPIVEIS

Box of Clues

Stumped? Maybe you can find a clue
below. (No clue for the mystery answer.)

-Combination of numbers and
 signs
-Arithmetic that combines
 letters and numbers
-Any of the numbers or symbols
 in math that, when multiplied
 together, form a product
-Natural _____
-Limit of the value of a function
 or variable when it tends to
 become numerically larger than
 any preassigned finite number
-Greater than zero

Arrange the circled letters
to solve the mystery answer.

MYSTERY ANSWER

THE HUMAN BODY

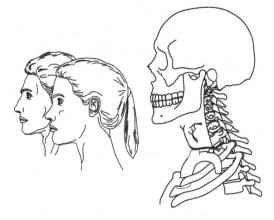

Unscramble the Jumbles, one letter
to each square, to spell words related
to the human body.

#1 SHETC

#2 LNEAK

#3 LPIEVS

#4 DIEYKN

#5 RTXOAH

#6 CSOAHTM

Interesting Human Body Facts

The average human eyelash survives about 150 days before falling out.

The average human heart beats about 100,000 times each day.

The average human scalp contains about 135,000 hairs.

Arrange the circled letters
to solve the mystery answer.

MYSTERY ANSWER

U.S. STATE CAPITALS

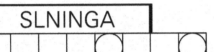

JUMBLE BrainBusters

Unscramble the Jumbles, one letter
to each square, to spell names of
U.S. state capitals.

#1 SLNINGA

#2 CILNLNO

#3 ROATRFDH

#4 NIRHOMDC

#5 MOCAULIB

#6 KRRAFNOTF

Box of Clues

Stumped? Maybe you can find a clue
below.

- Starts with *F*; ends with *T*
- Starts with *L*; ends with *N*
- Starts with *R*; ends with *D*
- Starts with *L*; ends with *G*
- Starts with *C*; ends with *A*
- Starts with *H*; ends with *D*
- Starts with *H*; ends with *G*

Arrange the circled letters
to solve the mystery answer.

MYSTERY ANSWER

MEANS THE SAME

JUMBLE BrainBusters

Unscramble the Jumbles, one letter to each square, to spell pairs of words that have the same or similar meanings.

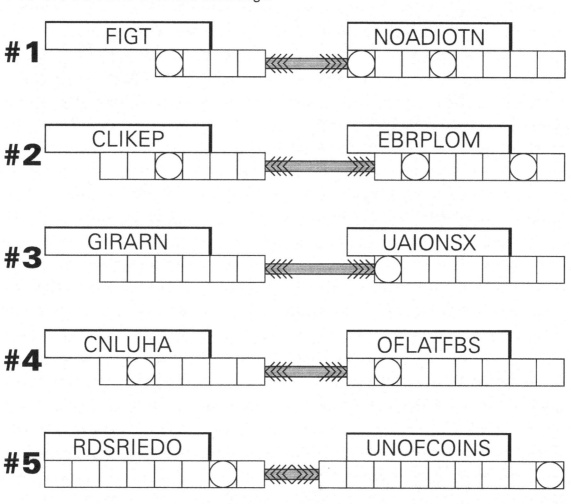

#1 FIGT   NOADIOTN

#2 CLIKEP   EBRPLOM

#3 GIRARN   UAIONSX

#4 CNLUHA   OFLATFBS

#5 RDSRIEDO   UNOFCOINS

Arrange the circled letters to solve the mystery answer.
(Form two words that have the same or similar meanings.)

MYSTERY ANSWER

TV SHOWS

JUMBLE BrainBusters

Unscramble the Jumbles, one letter to each square, to spell names of TV shows.

#1 SDNYATY

#2 NOBAZNA

Box of Clues

Stumped? Maybe you can find a clue below.

-Popular A.G. show
-ABC drama, 1981-1989
-Popular game show
-NBC show about a frontiersman
-Long-running Western
-Kate Jackson show, 1972-1976
-Popular ABC show, 1977-1986

#3 COAMLKT

#4 PDEJYOAR

#5 TKEHOREOIS

#6 ATEOBVEOTLH

Arrange the circled letters to solve the mystery answer.

MYSTERY ANSWER

WEATHER

Unscramble the Jumbles, one letter to each square, to spell words related to weather.

#1 ABIORS

#2 DNTERHU

#3 COENYLC

#4 NOABWIR

#5 OOMNSNO

#6 SREPUERS

Arrange the circled letters to solve the mystery answer.

Interesting Weather Fact

The invention and development of the telegraph in the mid-1800s made it possible to collect information from widespread weather stations, and thus enabled the first weather maps to be drawn.

MYSTERY ANSWER

SUPER JUMBLE® CHALLENGE

JUMBLE BrainBusters

Unscramble the Jumbles, one letter to each square, to spell words.

#1 OHG

#2 RTFU

#3 CDITH

#4 WTOLAU

#5 HGTHOTU

#6 BFOLOALT

#7 HMOAUTSHW

#8 ANHRIZOTLO

#9 KMSUREARETP

#10 OEABRVIATINB

Box of Clues

Stumped? Maybe you can find a clue below.

-Grass, roots, and some soil
-Liquid breath freshener
-Level to flat ground
-Large swine
-Make illegal
-Namath's sport
-Drainage _____
-Grocery store
-Uneasy
-Second _____
-Ave., to avenue

Arrange the circled letters to solve the mystery answer.

MYSTERY ANSWER

MEANS THE OPPOSITE

JUMBLE
BrainBusters

Unscramble the Jumbles, one letter
to each square, to spell pairs of words
that have opposite or nearly opposite
meanings.

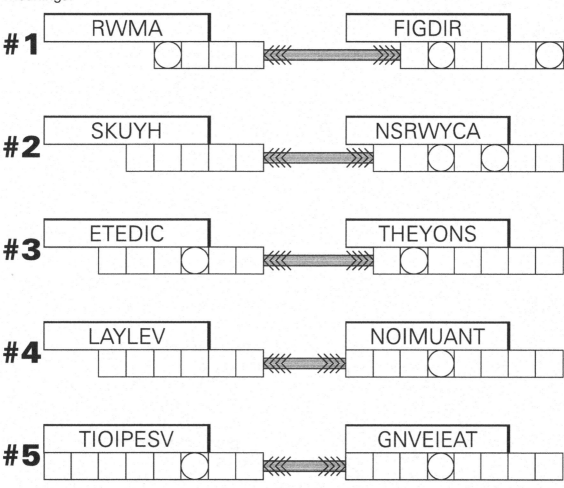

#1 RWMA   FIGDIR

#2 SKUYH   NSRWYCA

#3 ETEDIC   THEYONS

#4 LAYLEV   NOIMUANT

#5 TIOIPESV   GNVEIEAT

Arrange the circled letters to solve the mystery answer.
(Form two words that have the opposite or nearly
opposite meanings.)

MYSTERY
ANSWER

PLANET EARTH

Unscramble the Jumbles, one letter to each square, to spell words related to planet Earth.

#1 SBYSA

#2 HGULC

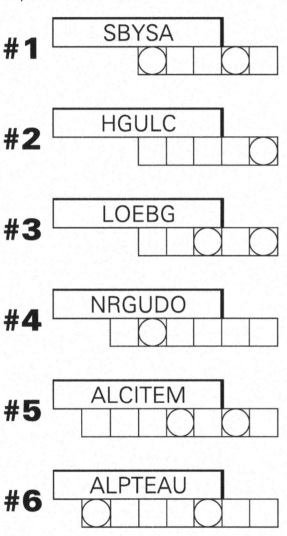

#3 LOEBG

#4 NRGUDO

#5 ALCITEM

#6 ALPTEAU

Box of Clues

Stumped? Maybe you can find a clue below. (No clue for the mystery answer.)

-Deep or precipitous cleft
-Weather conditions over a long period of time
-Surface
-Raised land area having a relatively level surface
-Deep gulf
-Spherical representation of the earth

Arrange the circled letters to solve the mystery answer.

MYSTERY ANSWER

STARTS WITH A VOWEL

JUMBLE BrainBusters

Unscramble the Jumbles, one letter to each square, to spell words that start with a vowel.

#1 OINR

#2 FUIYN

#3 GIAEM

#4 NOCEU

#5 DARAW

#6 CJOETB

#7 COCYPU

#8 SALOIHB

Box of Clues

Stumped? Maybe you can find a clue below.

- Do away with
- Picture
- Flatten, smooth out
- Inhabit
- Augment
- Bring together
- Prize
- Unit of weight
- Something material that may be perceived by the senses

Arrange the circled letters to solve the mystery answer.

MYSTERY ANSWER

MOVIES

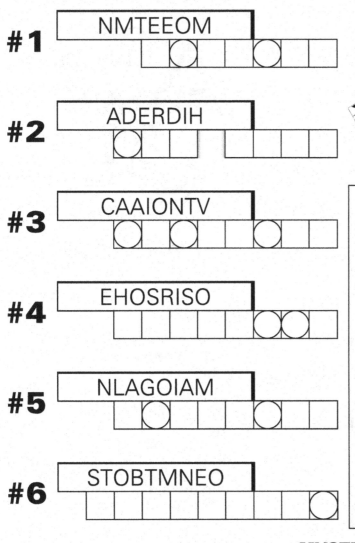

Unscramble the Jumbles, one letter to each square, to spell names of movies.

#1 NMTEEOM

#2 ADERDIH

#3 CAAIONTV

#4 EHOSRISO

#5 NLAGOIAM

#6 STOBTMNEO

Box of Clues

Stumped? Maybe you can find a clue below.

-Gene Hackman basketball movie
-1999 movie that shares its name with a tree
-1993 Western
-2000 movie about a man without any long-term memory
-1972 Burt Reynolds movie
-1983 Chevy Chase comedy
-1988 Bruce Willis movie

Arrange the circled letters to solve the mystery answer.

MYSTERY ANSWER

ATHLETES

JUMBLE.
BrainBusters

Unscramble the Jumbles, one letter to each square, to spell names of famous athletes.

#1 YT BCBO

#2 ACL NIPIKR

#3 GIYO RAREB

#4 FETFIS ARFG

#5 OJE ONATAMN

#6 TDE MIALISWL

Box of Clues

Stumped? Maybe you can find a clue below. (No clue for the mystery answer.)

- Yankees catcher and coach
- Popular quarterback
- Tigers player and manager
- Reliable Oriole
- German tennis player
- Red Sox player dubbed the "Splendid Splinter"

Arrange the circled letters to solve the mystery answer.

MYSTERY ANSWER

SPORTS

Unscramble the Jumbles, one letter to each square, to spell words related to sports.

#1 MOREH

#2 AIOLEG

#3 FEEDTA

#4 ASENOS

#5 TCVRYIO

#6 GAMAREN

Interesting Sports Facts

In 1934, Babe Ruth paid a fan $20 dollars for the return of the baseball he hit for his 700th career home run.

In the NFL, the home team is required to provide 24 footballs for each game.

Arrange the circled letters to solve the mystery answer.

MYSTERY ANSWER

TRIPLE JUMBLE® BRAINBUSTERS

JUMBLE® BrainBusters

Unscramble the Jumbles, one letter to each square, to spell words.

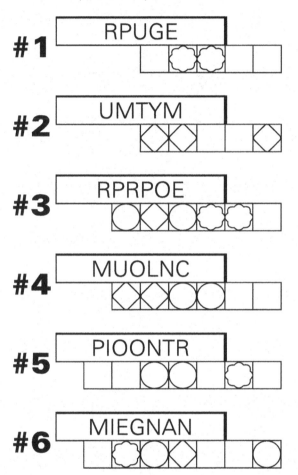

#1 RPUGE

#2 UMTYM

#3 RPRPOE

#4 MUOLNC

#5 PIOONTR

#6 MIEGNAN

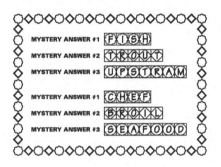

MYSTERY ANSWER #1 FISH
MYSTERY ANSWER #2 TROUT
MYSTERY ANSWER #3 UPSTRAM

MYSTERY ANSWER #1 CHEF
MYSTERY ANSWER #2 BROIL
MYSTERY ANSWER #3 SEAFOOD

Box of Clues

Stumped? Maybe you can find a clue below. (No clues for the mystery answers.)

- Part
- **Appropriate**
- **Steering** _____
- **Logical connotation**
- **Stomach**
- **Eliminate impurities**

Arrange the clouded letters to solve mystery answer #1. Arrange the diamonded letters to solve mystery answer #2. Arrange the circled letters to solve mystery answer #3.

(The mystery answers will relate to each other.)

MYSTERY ANSWER #1

MYSTERY ANSWER #2

MYSTERY ANSWER #3

ALL ABOUT MONEY

JUMBLE. BrainBusters

Unscramble the Jumbles, one letter to each square, to spell words related to money.

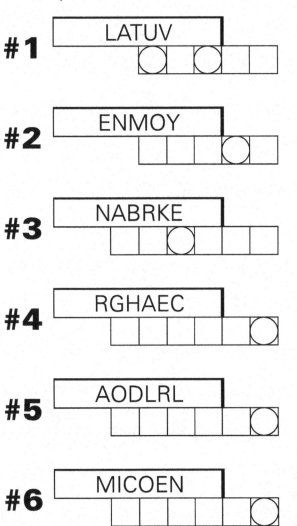

#1 LATUV

#2 ENMOY

#3 NABRKE

#4 RGHAEC

#5 AODLRL

#6 MICOEN

Interesting Money Fact

A study of American coins and currency revealed the presence of bacteria, including staphylococcus and E. coli, on about 18 percent of coins and 7 percent of bills.

Arrange the circled letters to solve the mystery answer.

MYSTERY ANSWER

JUMBLE TRIVIA

Unscramble the Jumbles, one letter to each square, to spell words as suggested by the trivia clues.

#1 This athlete's nickname was the "Iron Horse."

#1 REGIGH

#2 This is one of the fattiest fishes. Four ounces contain about nine grams of fat.

#2 MASNLO

#3 On the average, each American consumes about 120 pounds of _____ per year.

#3 OTPAEOST

#4 The average speed of an _____ is about 20 miles per hour.

#4 CANLVHAEA

#5 More of these occur in North America than on any other continent.

#5 NAOOREDST

Arrange the circled letters to solve the mystery answer.

The sale of chewing gum is outlawed in this country.

MYSTERY ANSWER ⭘⭘⭘⭘⭘⭘⭘⭘⭘

MOVIES

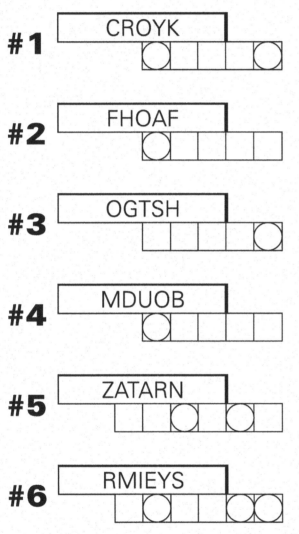

Unscramble the Jumbles, one letter
to each square, to spell names of
movies.

#1 CROYK

#2 FHOAF

#3 OGTSH

#4 MDUOB

#5 ZATARN

#6 RMIEYS

Arrange the circled letters
to solve the mystery answer.

JUMBLE BrainBusters

Interesting Movie Facts

Ronald Reagan's last acting
role before entering politics
was in the 1964 film *The
Killers*.

Sandra Bullock's role in
While You Were Sleeping
was originally offered to
Demi Moore, but her salary
demands were too high.

MYSTERY ANSWER

MATH

JUMBLE
BrainBusters

Unscramble the Jumbled
letters, one letter to each square,
so that each equation is correct.

For example: NWOLSOEPNEUTO
ONE PLUS ONE = TWO

#1 ETOULSSNENNVIEPW

☐☐☐☐ ☐☐◯◯☐ ☐☐☐☐☐☐ = ☐☐☐☐

#2 HNELTUREEFOSUOPR

☐☐☐☐ ☐☐◯☐ ☐☐☐☐☐◯ = ☐◯☐☐

#3 MTOTIUEFOSRETIHWG

◯☐☐☐ ☐☐☐◯☐ ☐☐☐☐☐ = ☐☐☐◯◯☐

#4 TMTENTISNUTNENWYE

☐☐☐◯☐☐ ☐◯☐☐◯ ☐☐☐ = ☐☐◯

#5 HNTERERITSHETEIEEMN

☐☐☐◯☐ ☐◯☐☐☐☐ ☐☐☐☐☐☐ = ☐☐◯☐

Then arrange the
circled letters to solve
the mystery equation.

MYSTERY EQUATION

◯◯◯ ◯◯◯◯◯ ◯◯◯◯◯◯ = ◯◯◯◯◯

WARS AND THE MILITARY

Unscramble the Jumbles, one letter to each square, to spell words related to wars and the military.

#1 MBBO

#2 SCAHL

#3 PEHOCRP

#4 HAISPWR

#5 TIFRANYN

#6 FCIOLTCN

Box of Clues

Stumped? Maybe you can find a clue below.

- Helicopter nickname
- Soldiers trained, armed, and equipped to fight on foot
- Japanese city home to Peace Memorial Park
- Fight, battle, war
- Atomic _____
- Naval vessel
- Hostile encounter

Arrange the circled letters to solve the mystery answer.

MYSTERY ANSWER

ADJECTIVES

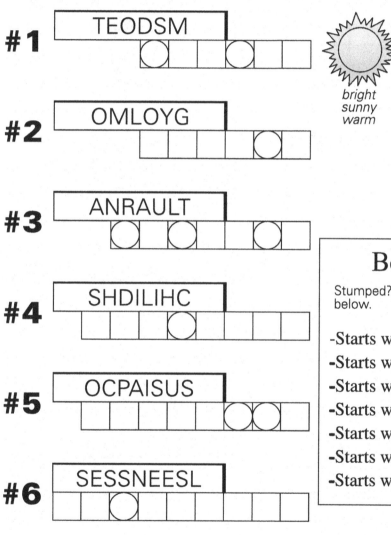

Unscramble the Jumbles, one letter
to each square, to spell adjectives.

#1 TEODSM

#2 OMLOYG

#3 ANRAULT

#4 SHDILIHC

#5 OCPAISUS

#6 SESSNEESL

bright
sunny
warm

large
African
Asian

strong
muscular
powerful

Box of Clues
Stumped? Maybe you can find a clue
below.

-Starts with *G*; ends with *Y*
-Starts with *S*; ends with *S*
-Starts with *M*; ends with *L*
-Starts with *C*; ends with *H*
-Starts with *M*; ends with *T*
-Starts with *N*; ends with *L*
-Starts with *S*; ends with *S*

Arrange the circled letters
to solve the mystery answer.

MYSTERY ANSWER

ANIMALS

JUMBLE BrainBusters

Unscramble the Jumbles, one letter to each square, to spell names of animals.

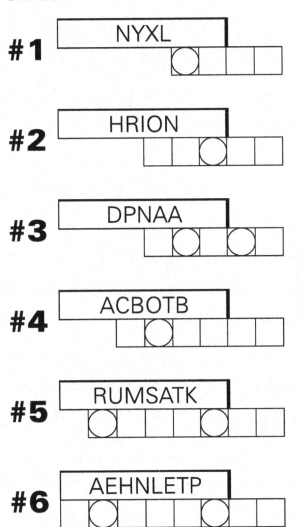

#1 NYXL

#2 HRION

#3 DPNAA

#4 ACBOTB

#5 RUMSATK

#6 AEHNLETP

Arrange the circled letters to solve the mystery answer.

★ **JUMBLE® Trivia** Quick Quiz

What plant-eating, slow-moving dugong relative can weigh as much as 1,500 pounds and live as long as 60 years?

ATEMNEA

ANSWER:

MYSTERY ANSWER

FOOD

JUMBLE BrainBusters

Unscramble the Jumbles, one letter to each square, to spell words related to food.

#1 REELYC

#2 LFWFEA

#3 MOTAOT

#4 GLAAANS

#5 LAEGPNTG

#6 CAWSDIHN

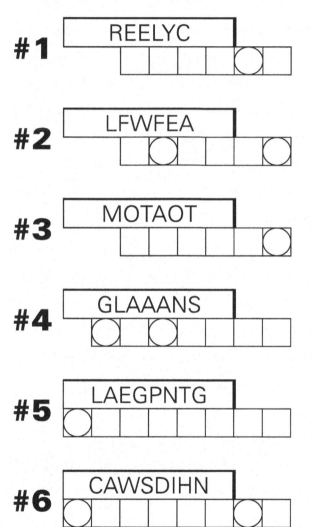

Interesting Food Facts

In ancient China and certain parts of India, mouse flesh was considered a delicacy.

In ancient Rome, flamingo tongues were considered a delicacy.

Arrange the circled letters to solve the mystery answer.

MYSTERY ANSWER

OUTER SPACE

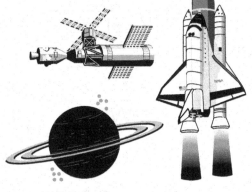

JUMBLE BrainBusters

Unscramble the Jumbles, one letter to each square, to spell words related to outer space.

#1 NUAUSR

#2 NELATP

#3 MOCOSS

#4 PENUETN

#5 REMCRYU

#6 NATSOROYM

Arrange the circled letters to solve the mystery answer.

Interesting Outer Space Facts

Scientists believe that hydrogen comprises about 90 to 99 percent of all matter in the universe.

Since Neptune's discovery in 1846, it has made only about three-quarters of one revolution around the Sun.

MYSTERY ANSWER

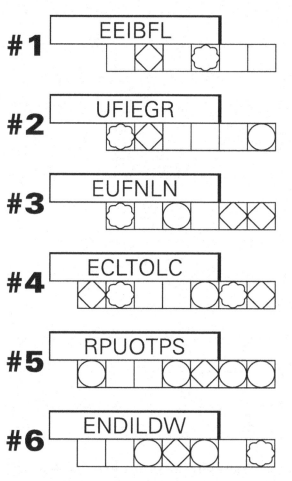

TRIPLE JUMBLE® BRAINBUSTERS

Unscramble the Jumbles, one letter to each square, to spell words.

#1 EEIBFL

#2 UFIEGR

#3 EUFNLN

#4 ECLTOLC

#5 RPUOTPS

#6 ENDILDW

JUMBLE BrainBusters

MYSTERY ANSWER #1 FISH
MYSTERY ANSWER #2 TROUT
MYSTERY ANSWER #3 UPSTREAM

MYSTERY ANSWER #1 CHEF
MYSTERY ANSWER #2 BROIL
MYSTERY ANSWER #3 SEAFOOD

Box of Clues

Stumped? Maybe you can find a clue below. (No clues for the mystery answers.)

-Credence
-Action _____
-Become steadily less
-Life _____
-Gather
-_____ cloud

Arrange the clouded letters to solve mystery answer #1. Arrange the diamonded letters to solve mystery answer #2. Arrange the circled letters to solve mystery answer #3.
(The mystery answers will relate to each other.)

MYSTERY ANSWER #1

MYSTERY ANSWER #2

MYSTERY ANSWER #3

BIRDS

Unscramble the Jumbles, one letter
to each square, to spell names of birds.

#1 CFNIH

#2 GELEA

#3 SOGOE

#4 OIGEPN

#5 EKTRYU

#6 COISRHT

Interesting Bird Facts

Studies have found that most ducks lay their eggs in the morning.

Albatrosses lay the heaviest eggs of any seabird

Bald eagles build the biggest nests of any bird. Some have measured 10 feet across.

Arrange the circled letters
to solve the mystery answer.

MYSTERY ANSWER

COUNTRIES

JUMBLE BrainBusters

Unscramble the Jumbles, one letter to each square, to spell names of countries.

#1 HCIEL

#2 DAFNLIN

#3 AOSLIAM

#4 RAUHNYG

#5 COMOORC

#6 AGOLTUPR

Arrange the circled letters to solve the mystery answer.

★ **JUMBLE Trivia** Quick Quiz

What country is home to the Bledowska Desert, Europe's only true desert?

OADPNL

ANSWER:

What country is divided into six states and two territories?

SUILRAAAT

ANSWER:

MYSTERY ANSWER

SUPER JUMBLE® CHALLENGE

JUMBLE. BrainBusters

Unscramble the Jumbles, one letter to each square, to spell words.

#1 PTE

#2 OUHR

#3 ESSEN

#4 FBEUTF

#5 POTUSCO

#6 NUSNHIES

#7 RCOCOAKHC

#8 OSBATEARDK

#9 MRGNHUIBDIM

#10 UHEGESEREBRC

Box of Clues

Stumped? Maybe you can find a clue below.

-Counter for refreshments
-Nocturnal insect
-Domesticated animal
-Plank mounted on wheels
-Brightly colored bird
-Powerful sea creature
-Common _____
-Perimeter of a circle
-Type of sandwich
-Star's bright output
-60 minutes

Arrange the circled letters to solve the mystery answer.

MYSTERY ANSWER

ANIMALS

JUMBLE BrainBusters

Unscramble the Jumbles, one letter to each square, to spell names of animals.

#1 TSOHL

#2 REFTRE

#3 AJAURG

#4 SEWALE

#5 FIRFEGA

#6 NLIEMGM

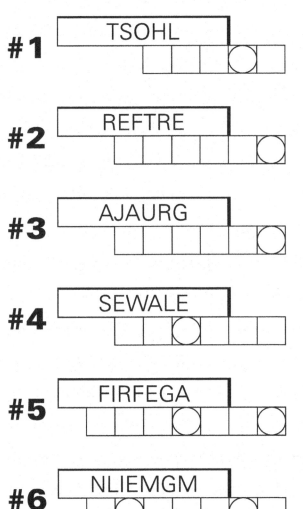

Interesting Animal Facts

It takes about 40 days for an ostrich egg to hatch.

Despite their humps, camels have straight spines.

It can take a deep-sea clam as long as 100 years to reach 0.3 inches in length

Arrange the circled letters to solve the mystery answer.

MYSTERY ANSWER

EUROPEAN COUNTRIES

Unscramble the Jumbles, one letter to each square, to spell names of European countries.

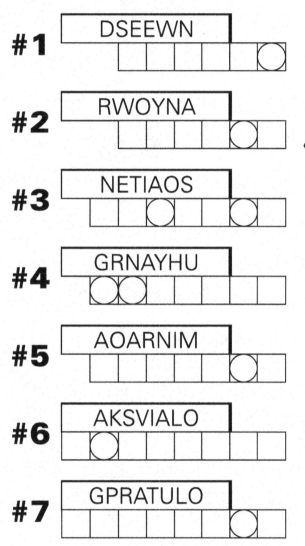

#1 DSEEWN

#2 RWOYNA

#3 NETIAOS

#4 GRNAYHU

#5 AOARNIM

#6 AKSVIALO

#7 GPRATULO

Arrange the circled letters to solve the mystery answer.

Box of Clues

Stumped? Maybe you can find a clue below.

-Starts with *S*; ends with *A*
-Starts with *H*; ends with *Y*
-Starts with *R*; ends with *A*
-Starts with *P*; ends with *L*
-Starts with *E*; ends with *A*
-Starts with *S*; ends with *N*
-Starts with *L*; ends with *A*
-Starts with *N*; ends with *Y*

MYSTERY ANSWER

WARS AND THE MILITARY

Unscramble the Jumbles, one letter to each square, to spell words related to wars and the military.

#1 ARTDF

#2 CTKATA

#3 NAECENT

#4 RUAMAIS

#5 SGORRINA

#6 TDSREOERY

Box of Clues

Stumped? Maybe you can find a clue below.

- Military retainer of a Japanese daimyo practicing the code of conduct of Bushido
- Permanent military installation
- System for selecting individuals for military service
- Large-scale U.S. operation in the Persian Gulf War
- Offensive military action
- Small, fast warship used especially to support larger vessels
- Soldier's container for liquid

Arrange the circled letters to solve the mystery answer.

MYSTERY ANSWER

TRIPLE JUMBLE® BRAINBUSTERS

Unscramble the Jumbles, one letter to each square, to spell words.

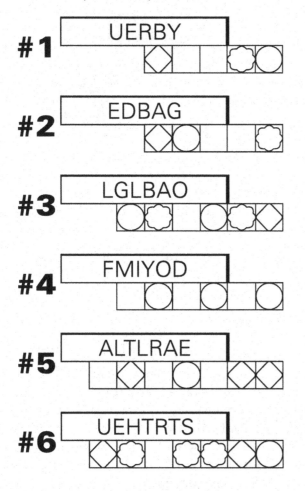

#1 UERBY

#2 EDBAG

#3 LGLBAO

#4 FMIYOD

#5 ALTLRAE

#6 UEHTRTS

MYSTERY ANSWER #1 F I S H
MYSTERY ANSWER #2 T R O U T
MYSTERY ANSWER #3 U P S T R A M

MYSTERY ANSWER #1 C H E F
MYSTERY ANSWER #2 B R O I L
MYSTERY ANSWER #3 S E A F O O D

Box of Clues

Stumped? Maybe you can find a clue below. (No clues for the mystery answers.)

-Horizontal
-Awarded emblem
-Worldwide
-Purchaser
-Change
-Movable louver

Arrange the clouded letters to solve mystery answer #1. Arrange the diamonded letters to solve mystery answer #2. Arrange the circled letters to solve mystery answer #3.
(The mystery answers will relate to each other.)

MYSTERY ANSWER #1

MYSTERY ANSWER #2

MYSTERY ANSWER #3

PLANET EARTH

Unscramble the Jumbles, one letter to each square, to spell words related to planet Earth.

#1 LILH

#2 ERCKE

#3 NAILDS

#4 LAEYLV

#5 LGJNEU

#6 NUTARD

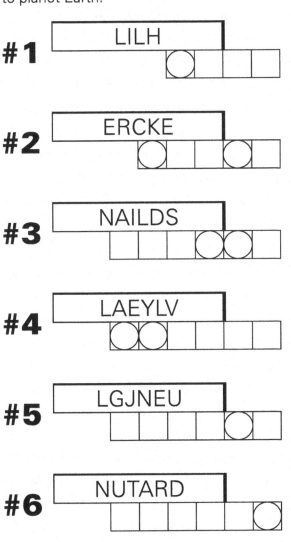

Interesting Planet Earth Facts

There are about 50 geyser fields known to exist on Earth.

One gallon of seawater contains about one quarter-pound of salt.

The Agulhas current, in the western Indian Ocean, is the fastest ocean current in the world.

Arrange the circled letters to solve the mystery answer.

MYSTERY ANSWER

MATH

JUMBLE BrainBusters

Unscramble the Jumbled letters, one letter to each square, so that each equation is correct.

For example: NWOLSOEPNEUTO
ONE PLUS ONE = TWO

#1 OSTOUUFEDRQARW

#2 GOFUPRLUFEIHTRSUO

#3 MRINNEINSIEENONUZ

#4 VFWNSVNEIUSIETOEM

#5 ETHMTREIETRENNEIHES

Then arrange the circled letters to solve the mystery equation.

MYSTERY EQUATION

SUPER JUMBLE® CHALLENGE

JUMBLE.
BrainBusters

Unscramble the Jumbles, one letter
to each square, to spell words.

#1 MMO

#2 XEIT

#3 ELHOL

#4 INIBIK

#5 SMAIVES

#6 DSOLUERH

#7 HEOBKSLFO

#8 METAHEANRW

#9 NAIDERSIVGT

#10 RRTUNDSOMTHE

Box of Clues

Stumped? Maybe you can find a clue below.

-Powerful weather disturbance
-Promoting, notifying
-Novel supporter
-Cold _____
-Skimpy swimsuit
-Emergency _____
-Huge
-Forecaster
-Hi
-Memorable
-Mother

Arrange the circled
letters to solve the
mystery answer.

MYSTERY ANSWER

AUTOMOBILES

JUMBLE BrainBusters

Unscramble the Jumbles, one letter to each square, to spell words related to automobiles.

#1 OHDO

#2 UNRKT

#3 ACHUPB

#4 HVICELE

#5 HSCSIAS

#6 RATBTYE

#7 GEILEMA

#8 TIOINING

#9 MOROEETD

Arrange the circled letters to solve the mystery answer.

MYSTERY ANSWER

SPORTS

**JUMBLE®
BrainBusters**

Unscramble the Jumbles, one letter
to each square, to spell words related
to sports.

#1 GNININ

#2 NINSTE

#3 NOBIGX

#4 CHEYOK

#5 LBFEMU

#6 SNEDEEF

#7 CHTAREC

#8 DSIUMTA

#9 SLBBALAE

Arrange the circled
letters to solve the
mystery answer.

MYSTERY ANSWER

ANIMALS

JUMBLE BrainBusters

Unscramble the Jumbles, one letter to each square, to spell words related to animals.

#1 YHEAN

#2 ANADP

#3 AOKAL

#4 MSPRIH

#5 EASWLE

#6 TEAPNRH

#7 SAMUKTR

#8 LBWLAYA

#9 PLAETOEN

#10 RKAOONGA

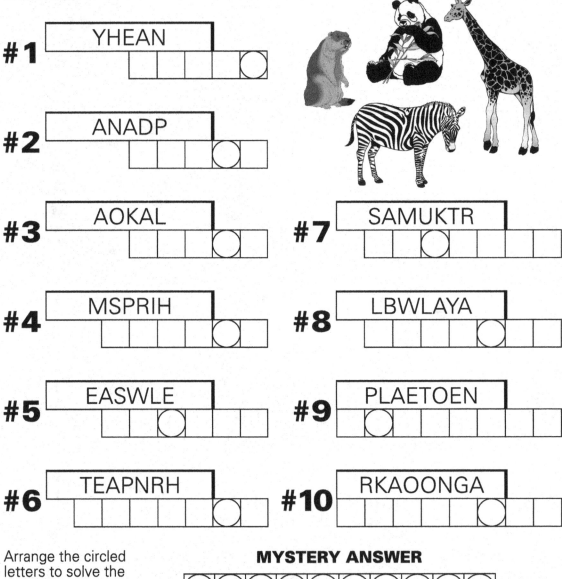

Arrange the circled letters to solve the mystery answer.

MYSTERY ANSWER

OCCUPATIONS

Unscramble the Jumbles, one letter to each square, to spell names of occupations.

#1 EHFC

#2 UTDEYP

#3 OKBERR

#4 TAIRWE

#5 REWIRT

#6 CODTRO

#7 TOAIRJN

#8 MSCEITH

#9 CRBUHET

#10 CAMENICH

Arrange the circled letters to solve the mystery answer.

MYSTERY ANSWER

FOOD

Unscramble the Jumbles, one letter to each square, to spell words related to food.

#1 VRYGA

#2 GFUED

#3 NHOYE

#4 RCEEYL

#5 GLAANAS

#6 KCRCERA

#7 TRCUDSA

#8 AOCELSWL

#9 LAEMBLAT

#10 DASWNCIH

Arrange the circled letters to solve the mystery answer.

MYSTERY ANSWER

PUZZLE 176

ASTRONOMY

JUMBLE BrainBusters

Unscramble the Jumbles, one letter to each square, to spell words related to outer space.

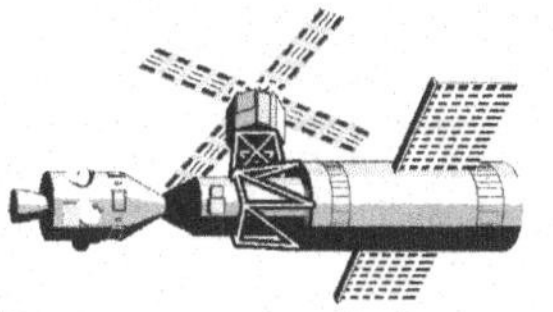

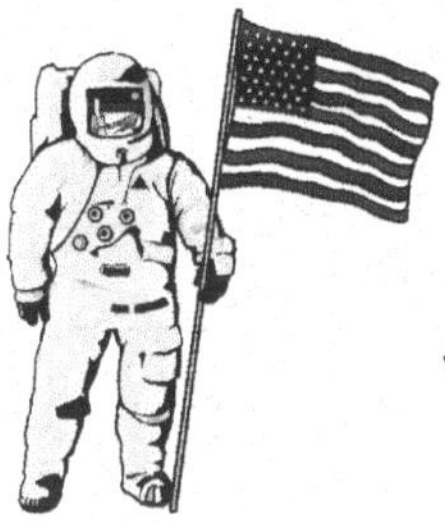

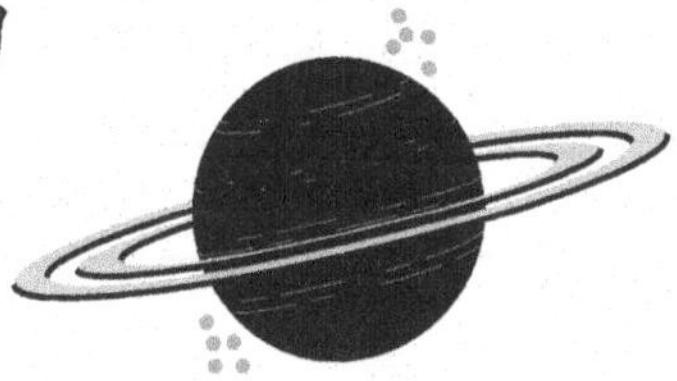

#1 RIOTB

#2 LUOTP

#3 OCTME

#4 XYGLAA

#5 RUATNS

#6 AUUSNR

#7 PJEIRTU

#8 NNEUETP

#9 URECYMR

#10 RATDEOIS

Arrange the circled letters to solve the mystery answer.

MYSTERY ANSWER

WEATHER

JUMBLE BrainBusters

Unscramble the Jumbles, one letter to each square, to spell words related to weather.

#1 ADPM

#2 ONWS

#3 NYSNU

#4 NWYID

#5 UIHDM

#6 EREEFZ

#7 MTLIAEC

#8 STETIRW

#9 GHDOTRU

#10 LFARANIL

Arrange the circled letters to solve the mystery answer.

MYSTERY ANSWER

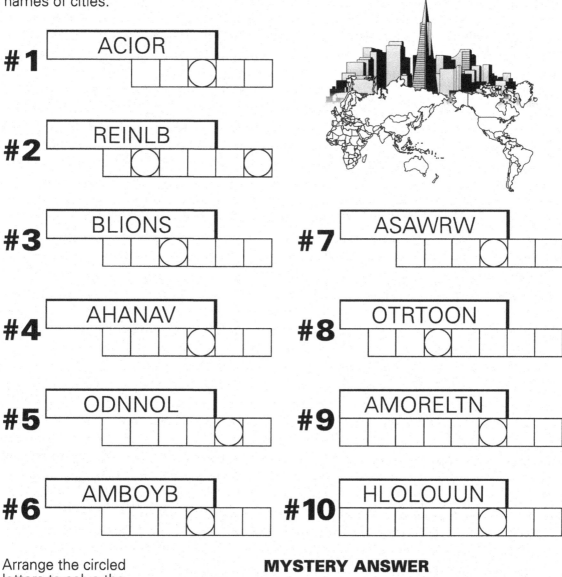

PUZZLE 178

CITIES

JUMBLE BrainBusters

Unscramble the Jumbles, one letter to each square, to spell names of cities.

#1 ACIOR

#2 REINLB

#3 BLIONS

#4 AHANAV

#5 ODNNOL

#6 AMBOYB

#7 ASAWRW

#8 OTRTOON

#9 AMORELTN

#10 HLOLOUUN

Arrange the circled letters to solve the mystery answer.

MYSTERY ANSWER

ANSWERS

1. **Jumbles:** #1 OBOE #2 PIANO #3 BANJO #4 VIOLIN #5 GUITAR #6 CONCERT
Answer: CLARINET
2. **Jumbles:** #1 CANADA #2 OSTRICH #3 PRESLEY #4 MATCHES #5 GREENLAND
Answer: DISNEYLAND
3. **Jumbles:** #1 DAVE #2 HEIST #3 SHREK #4 TWINS #5 CONTACT #6 MAVERICK
Answer: INSOMNIA
4. **Jumbles:** #1 DUCK #2 CRAB #3 FROG #4 TIGER #5 SKUNK #6 OTTER
Answer: RACCOON
5. **Jumbles:** #1 LIKE BIKE #2 LAZY HAZY #3 DAMP CRAMP #4 FLING SPRING #5 EIGHT WEIGHT
Answer: CAKE FAKE
6. **Jumbles:** #1 IOWA #2 IDAHO #3 MAINE #4 ALASKA #5 NEVADA #6 NEBRASKA
Answer: ALABAMA
7. **Jumbles:** #1 SOAP #2 ALICE #3 COACH #4 FAMILY #5 HUNTER #6 BENSON
Answer: COLUMBO
8. **Jumbles:** #1 BOLD #2 BUNNY #3 BABOON #4 BENEFIT #5 BARGAIN #6 BURGLAR #7 BROTHER #8 BALLOON
Answer: BUILDING
9. **Jumbles:** #1 ORBIT #2 COMET #3 PLANET #4 SATURN #5 GALAXY #6 JUPITER
Answer: MERCURY
10. **Jumbles:** #1 ZINC #2 COBALT #3 SULFUR #4 COPPER #5 HELIUM #6 URANIUM
Answer: CALCIUM
11. **Jumbles:** #1 ENGINE #2 HUBCAP #3 CLUTCH #4 BUMPER #5 MUFFLER #6 WARRANTY
Answer: BATTERY
12. **Jumbles:** #1 FIGHT #2 TRIPLE #3 INNING #4 TENNIS #5 HOCKEY #6 FUMBLE
Answer: OFFENSE
13. **Jumbles:** #1 VENT #2 FLOOR #3 PANTRY #4 WINDOW #5 CHIMNEY #6 BASEMENT
Answer: DRIVEWAY
14. **Jumbles:** #1 APEX #2 AGAIN #3 EJECT #4 INVADE #5 INJURY #6 EFFORT #7 ACTION #8 URGENT
Answer: ACTIVATE
15. **Jumbles:** #1 RIVER #2 BEACH #3 SWAMP #4 TRENCH #5 GROUND #6 VOLCANO
Answer: MOUNTAIN
16. **Jumbles:** #1 PAYMENTS #2 SOONER #3 MAKES #4 EASY #5 FORTUNATE
Answer: MONEY
17. **Jumbles:** #1 BLAST #2 PEACE #3 COUNT #4 HUNCH #5 HUMAN #6 BOTTOM
Answer: #1 BEACH #2 SUNTAN
18. **Jumbles:** #1 FACT FICTION #2 GLAD UNHAPPY #3 LOSS VICTORY #4 MORON GENIUS #5 BLEAK CHEERFUL
Answer: BACK FRONT
19. **Jumbles:** #1 SHINY #2 BALMY #3 MIGHTY #4 MELODY #5 JOURNEY #6 CUSTODY
Answer: SUMMARY
20. **Jumbles:** #1 CASH #2 EURO #3 MINT #4 VAULT #5 PENNY #6 LENDER
Answer: PAYMENT
21. **Jumbles:** #1 FISH #2 PORK #3 FRUIT #4 SALAD #5 FUDGE #6 BACON
Answer: PUDDING
22. **Jumbles:** #1 WARM #2 SLUSH #3 RADAR #4 WINDY #5 CLOUDY #6 TWISTER
Answer: HUMIDITY
23. **Jumbles:** #1 BOISE #2 AUSTIN #3 ALBANY #4 PHOENIX #5 LINCOLN #6 ATLANTA
Answer: BOSTON
24. **Jumbles:** #1 CHEF #2 PILOT #3 COACH #4 DOCTOR #5 WAITER #6 JANITOR
Answer: ARCHITECT
25. **Jumbles:** #1 DULL #2 PLAIN #3 NOBLE #4 ROOMY #5 STUPID #6 BRIGHT
Answer: SUPERB
26. **Jumbles:** #1 INDIA #2 JAPAN #3 EGYPT #4 BRAZIL #5 FRANCE #6 POLAND
Answer: ENGLAND
27. **Jumbles:** #1 HEAD #2 NECK #3 LUNG #4 FOOT #5 THUMB #6 MOUTH
Answer: TONGUE
28. **Jumbles:** #1 TAFT #2 FORD #3 NIXON #4 GRANT #5 ADAMS #6 HOOVER
Answer: REAGAN
29. **Jumbles:** #1 PENNY #2 FETCH #3 KNIGHT #4 JESTER #5 FATHER #6 NARROW
Answer: #1 JAPAN #2 ORIENT
30. **Jumbles:** #1 PUSH IMPEL #2 GROW EXPAND #3 HARM DAMAGE #4 BASIC PRIMARY #5 BRUTAL SAVAGE
Answer: BOLD BRAVE
31. **Jumbles:** #1 FISH #2 MOLE #3 EAGLE #4 WHALE #5 TURTLE #6 CHICKEN
Answer: CHEETAH
32. **Jumbles:** #1 SLICE #2 EAGLE #3 DRIVER #4 HAZARD #5 PALMER #6 NORMAN
Answer: HANDICAP
33. **Jumbles:** #1 MAUDE #2 EMERIL #3 BECKER #4 CHEERS #5 FLIPPER #6 NEWHART
Answer: BEWITCHED
34. **Jumbles:** #1 BEEF #2 PIZZA #3 SUGAR #4 PICKLE #5 TURKEY #6 CHEESE
Answer: BISCUIT
35. **Jumbles:** #1 SUNK TRUNK #2 CASED PLACED #3 SICKLE PICKLE #4 PILLOW WILLOW #5 COMBAT WOMBAT
Answer: MIND BLIND
36. **Jumbles:** #1 RUGBY #2 ERROR #3 COACH #4 SKIING #5 HELMET #6 FAIRWAY
Answer: UNIFORM
37. **Jumbles:** #1 LIGHT #2 CABLE #3 PAPER #4 MARRY #5 MOUTH #6 INCOME
Answer: #1 MAMMAL #2 ELEPHANT
38. **Jumbles:** #1 WHALE #2 ALASKA #3 SAHARA #4 CANADA #5 PACIFIC #6 JUPITER
Answer: ELEPHANT
39. **Jumbles:** #1 MORNING #2 JOLTED #3 TRUCK #4 DRIFT #5 PHONE #6 NUMBER
Answer: COMMOTION
40. **Jumbles:** #1 GIVEN #2 GUILTY #3 GENIUS #4 GOSSIP #5 GROUND #6 GROWTH #7 GARBAGE #8 GRAMMAR
Answer: GOVERNOR

41. **Jumbles:** #1 FARGO #2 JUNIOR #3 CASINO
#4 ARTHUR #5 TOOTSIE #6 AIRPLANE
Answer: TOP GUN

42. **Jumbles:** #1 TEN – FIVE = FIVE
#2 SIX + SIX = TWELVE
#3 TWO + SEVEN = NINE
#4 ZERO + ZERO = ZERO
#5 EIGHT – FOUR = FOUR
Answer: TWO + ZERO = TWO

43. **Jumbles:** #1 PLUTO #2 PROBE #3 URANUS
#4 PLANET #5 JUPITER #6 HYDROGEN
Answer: ASTEROIDS

44. **Jumbles:** #1 BUNNY HONEY #2 CLAIM
FRAME #3 TAKEN SHAKEN #4 SUMMER
BUMMER #5 JUMBLE CRUMBLE
Answer: BERRY MERRY

45. **Jumbles:** #1 RUSSIA #2 GREECE #3 MEXICO
#4 IRELAND #5 ROMANIA #6 PAKISTAN
Answer: DENMARK

46. **Jumbles:** #1 BACH #2 SONG #3 FLUTE
#4 TEMPO #5 BEATLES #6 TRUMPET
Answer: MEASURE

47. **Jumbles:** #1 BARBIE #2 KANGAROO
#3 BALLPOINT #4 JEFFERSON
#5 ESCALATOR
Answer: JINGLE BELLS

48. **Jumbles:** #1 CAKE #2 JELLY #3 GRAVY
#4 BUTTER #5 SHRIMP #6 CRACKER
Answer: HAMBURGER

49. **Jumbles:** #1 OHIO #2 KANSAS #3 OREGON
#4 WYOMING #5 VERMONT #6 COLORADO
Answer: MONTANA

50. **Jumbles:** #1 HAIL #2 SNOW #3 STORM
#4 DEGREE #5 STRATUS #6 DOWNPOUR
Answer: SUNSHINE

51. **Jumbles:** #1 FRAME #2 PICKUP #3 ENGINE
#4 VEHICLE #5 CHASSIS #6 ODOMETER
Answer: HEADLIGHTS

52. **Jumbles:** #1 ORDER #2 CROWD #3 GROOM
#4 BRIGHT #5 PUDDLE #6 MANNER
Answer: #1 WATER #2 COMPOUND

53. **Jumbles:** #1 TAXI #2 HOTEL #3 KUNG FU
#4 FRASIER #5 STAR TREK #6 GOOD TIMES
Answer: THE MONKEES

54. **Jumbles:** #1 CURVE #2 COACH #3 STRIKE
#4 DUGOUT #5 WARNING #6 DIAMOND
Answer: CATCHER

55. **Jumbles:** #1 LAVA #2 BLUFF #3 GRASS
#4 VALLEY #5 WINTER #6 LAGOON
Answer: WATERFALL

56. **Jumbles:** #1 SHAKY #2 WACKY #3 UNEASY
#4 PLENTY #5 FACTORY #6 LAUNDRY
Answer: CAUSEWAY

57. **Jumbles:** #1 GIVE PROVIDE #2 WISE
PRUDENT #3 HUMAN PERSON #4 FREELY
EASILY #5 GIGGLE CHUCKLE
Answer: WELL HEALTHY

58. **Jumbles:** #1 NURSE #2 TAILOR #3 AUTHOR
#4 BROKER #5 REALTOR #6 PLUMBER
Answer: ASTRONAUT

59. **Jumbles:** #1 PUMA #2 HYENA #3 LLAMA
#4 MOUSE #5 TURKEY #6 WALRUS
Answer: WEASEL

60. **Jumbles:** #1 IDIOT #2 ABYSS #3 ENJOY
#4 EXCITE #5 UNTRUE #6 ESCAPE
#7 IMPACT #8 ACROSS
Answer: ACCIDENT

61. **Jumbles:** #1 POLK #2 NIXON #3 ARTHUR
#4 WILSON #5 KENNEDY #6 JACKSON
Answer: JOHNSON

62. **Jumbles:** #1 TINY #2 FISHY #3 DARING
#4 HORRID #5 FEEBLE #6 JOYFUL
Answer: INFERIOR

63. **Jumbles:** #1 NAVY #2 SIEGE #3 FRONT
#4 WEAPON #5 OFFICER #6 COLONEL
Answer: INVASION

64. **Jumbles:** #1 WORK PLAY #2 FINAL INITIAL
#3 PEACE WARTIME #4 STURDY FLIMSY
#5 DIVIDE MULTIPLY
Answer: SICK WELL

65. **Jumbles:** #1 JOINT #2 PULSE #3 TOOTH
#4 BLOOD #5 ARTERY #6 MUSCLE
Answer: STOMACH

66. **Jumbles:** #1 EIGHT ÷ TWO = FOUR
#2 TWENTY – TEN = TEN
#3 FOUR + FOUR = EIGHT
#4 THIRTY x TWO = SIXTY
#5 EIGHT – EIGHT = ZERO
Answer: THREE x THREE = NINE

67. **Jumbles:** #1 LIGHT #2 PANTRY #3 CLOSET
#4 CEILING #5 FREEZER #6 BATHTUB
Answer: BLUEPRINTS

68. **Jumbles:** #1 HELENA #2 JUNEAU #3 RALEIGH
#4 JACKSON #5 BISMARCK #6 COLUMBUS
Answer: LANSING

69. **Jumbles:** #1 IRON #2 GOLD #3 OXYGEN
#4 HELIUM #5 SODIUM #6 MERCURY
Answer: HYDROGEN

70. **Jumbles:** #1 GOWN #2 OUTFIT #3 JACKET
#4 SHORTS #5 TUXEDO #6 APPAREL
Answer: SWEATER

71. **Jumbles:** #1 LOAN #2 PENNY #3 STOCK
#4 INVEST #5 CHARGE #6 BILLFOLD
Answer: SAVINGS

72. **Jumbles:** #1 DATA #2 MENU #3 MOUSE
#4 LAPTOP #5 MEMORY #6 MONITOR
Answer: INTERNET

73. **Jumbles:** #1 MITT #2 CATCH #3 STRIKE
#4 JERSEY #5 HUDDLE #6 PITCHER
Answer: STADIUM

74. **Jumbles:** #1 CRUSH #2 DOUGH #3 WITCH
#4 FROWN #5 LITTER #6 THRONG
Answer: #1 OUTFIT #2 CLOTHING

75. **Jumbles:** #1 HAZY CRAZY #2 DUMP TRUMP
#3 TRICK BRICK #4 SINGE CRINGE
#5 DOUBLE TROUBLE
Answer: DUCK TRUCK

76. **Jumbles:** #1 EPIC #2 UNFIT #3 ISSUE
#4 UNCLE #5 EMPTY #6 ORIGIN #7 EXPORT
#8 ANXIETY
Answer: OPTICIAN

77. **Jumbles:** #1 DALLAS #2 CANNON #3 MANNIX
#4 PHYLLIS #5 THE SAINT #6 GET SMART
Answer: LOST IN SPACE

78. **Jumbles:** #1 FRY #2 FLAG #3 FORCE
#4 SUPPLY #5 BLEMISH #6 PROVINCE
#7 SUNFLOWER #8 MICROSCOPE
#9 RESIGNATION #10 THOROUGHBRED
Answer: ADVERTISEMENT

79. **Jumbles:** #1 MUFFIN #2 SHRIMP
#3 PUDDING #4 CHICKEN #5 COCONUT
#6 MEATBALL
Answer: FROSTING

80. **Jumbles:** #1 DRILL #2 FRONT #3 DECAY
#4 LOOSE #5 TIRADE #6 REFUSE
Answer: #1 CITY #2 ORLANDO #3 FLORIDA

81. **Jumbles:** #1 SIX – SIX = ZERO
#2 FIVE + FIVE = TEN
#3 THREE ÷ ONE = THREE
#4 FIFTY – FIFTY = ZERO
#5 TWELVE – SEVEN = FIVE
Answer: TWO + NINE = ELEVEN

82. **Jumbles:** #1 FLORIDA #2 ARIZONA
#3 GEORGIA #4 VIRGINIA #5 ILLINOIS
#6 NEBRASKA
Answer: ARKANSAS

83. **Jumbles:** #1 HIPPO #2 RABBIT #3 SHRIMP
#4 MONKEY #5 GRIZZLY #6 PANTHER
Answer: TORTOISE

84. **Jumbles:** #1 SMIRK #2 MERCY #3 KITTEN
#4 SWATCH #5 CUSTOM #6 CORRECT
Answer: #1 SCIENCE #2 CHEMISTRY

85. **Jumbles:** #1 DOVE #2 ROBIN #3 PENGUIN
#4 VULTURE #5 BUZZARD #6 SPARROW
Answer: BLUEBIRD

86. **Jumbles:** #1 PUNT #2 COACH #3 BROWN
#4 TACKLE #5 HUDDLE #6 FUMBLE
Answer: TOUCHDOWN

87. **Jumbles:** #1 HABIT #2 PRIME #3 AGENT
#4 UNJUST #5 ROTTEN #6 GOBBLE
Answer: #1 PERSON #2 HUMAN BEING

88. **Jumbles:** #1 GRANT #2 BOXING #3 BOLIVIA
#4 THUNDER #5 SHORTHAND
Answer: HOT DOG VENDORS

89. **Jumbles:** #1 KOALA #2 SLOTH #3 LIZARD
#4 JACKAL #5 COYOTE #6 GOPHER
Answer: CROCODILE

90. **Jumbles:** #1 WEBSTER #2 SURVIVOR
#3 ROSEANNE #4 DINOSAURS #5 MIAMI VICE
#6 EMPTY NEST
Answer: PROVIDENCE

91. **Jumbles:** #1 PULSE #2 GLAND #3 SPLEEN
#4 THROAT #5 ANATOMY #6 SKELETON
Answer: ESOPHAGUS

92. **Jumbles:** #1 SUNNY CLOUDY
#2 TARDY PROMPT #3 FINISH COMMENCE
#4 RELEASE CAPTURE
#5 NERVOUS RELAXED
Answer: LOSS PROFIT

93. **Jumbles:** #1 TEN – TEN = ZERO
#2 TWO x ZERO = ZERO
#3 TWELVE – SIX = SIX
#4 SEVEN + TWO = NINE
#5 FIVE + SIX = ELEVEN
Answer: SEVEN – FIVE = TWO

94. **Jumbles:** #1 FOLLY #2 TRUTH #3 FUTURE
#4 TOMORROW #5 OBLIGED #6 BEHIND
Answer: LIFETIME

95. **Jumbles:** #1 PATIO #2 PORCH #3 SIDING
#4 WINDOW #5 BALCONY #6 PLUMBING
Answer: DINING ROOM

96. **Jumbles:** #1 DIGIT #2 RATIO #3 MINUS
#4 ANSWER #5 PRODUCT #6 DIVISION
Answer: ADDITION

97. **Jumbles:** #1 EASY #2 AWAY #3 OFFER
#4 INTACT #5 UNEVEN #6 AFFORD
#7 ABACUS #8 IMMUNE
Answer: OVERCAST

98. **Jumbles:** #1 CHECK #2 WALLET #3 RECEIPT
#4 FINANCE #5 CLOSING #6 CURRENCY
Answer: INTEREST

99. **Jumbles:** #1 GUY #2 HALF #3 PLANK
#4 FUSION #5 SHUTTLE #6 MORTGAGE
#7 SANDPAPER #8 BEFOREHAND
#9 CHEERLEADER #10 TRANSMISSION
Answer: HEARTBREAKING

100. **Jumbles:** #1 MINGLE #2 METHOD
#3 MOMENT #4 MACHINE #5 MAILBOX
#6 MYSTERY #7 MEASURE #8 MANAGER
Answer: MORTGAGE

101. **Jumbles:** #1 TREATY #2 DEFECT #3 PRIVATE
#4 ADMIRAL #5 WARFARE #6 INVASION
Answer: VETERANS

102. **Jumbles:** #1 NOISY #2 MANLY #3 VICIOUS
#4 INTENSE #5 FRIENDLY #6 IGNORANT
Answer: FANTASTIC

103. **Jumbles:** #1 TAFT #2 HAYES #3 ARTHUR
#4 REAGAN #5 LINCOLN #6 HARDING
Answer: GARFIELD

104. **Jumbles:** #1 KINGPIN #2 BANDITS
#3 PAYBACK #4 THE MASK #5 GODZILLA
#6 SUPERMAN
Answer: ARMAGEDDON

105. **Jumbles:** #1 ORBIT #2 PLUTO #3 ECLIPSE
#4 JUPITER #5 GRAVITY #6 SUNSPOT
Answer: SATELLITE

106. **Jumbles:** #1 ONE x ONE = ONE
#2 FOUR ÷ TWO = TWO
#3 SIX + THREE = NINE
#4 FOUR x TWO = EIGHT
#5 SEVEN – SEVEN = ZERO
Answer: TWO + TWO = EIGHT – FOUR

107. **Jumbles:** #1 ITALY #2 KENYA #3 ICELAND
#4 ETHIOPIA #5 THAILAND #6 COLOMBIA
Answer: CAMBODIA

108. **Jumbles:** #1 BARBER #2 BANKER
#3 CASHIER #4 FIREMAN #5 JEWELER
#6 SURGEON
Answer: ENGINEER

109. **Jumbles:** #1 HARP #2 SONG #3 ALBUM
#4 MOZART #5 MELODY #6 CONCERT
Answer: ORCHESTRA

110. **Jumbles:** #1 PIERRE #2 TOPEKA #3 BOSTON
#4 OLYMPIA #5 CONCORD #6 HONOLULU
Answer: ANNAPOLIS

111. **Jumbles:** #1 CLEAR SUNNY
#2 CARRY TRANSPORT #3 BLAZING BURNING
#4 EXPLAIN JUSTIFY #5 VICTORY TRIUMPH
Answer: TRIP JOURNEY

112. **Jumbles:** #1 OZONE #2 RUMBA #3 INVENT
#4 NEBULA #5 PICTURE #6 PRODUCT
Answer: #1 MOVIE #2 POPCORN
#3 AUDIENCE

113. **Jumbles:** #1 TRUNK #2 RADIO #3 COUPE
#4 PICKUP #5 TRAFFIC #6 WINDOWS
Answer: INSURANCE

114. **Jumbles:** #1 GLOVE #2 TENNIS #3 ROOKIE
#4 DOUBLE #5 FAIRWAY #6 DIAMOND
Answer: WRESTLING

115. **Jumbles:** #1 IMPLY #2 TACKY #3 SNOWY #4 TOUCHY #5 FINICKY #6 HICKORY
Answer: INSTANTLY

116. **Jumbles:** #1 IODINE #2 COPPER #3 SILICON #4 CALCIUM #5 NITROGEN #6 ALUMINUM
Answer: PLUTONIUM

117. **Jumbles:** #1 BYTE #2 CLICK #3 DELETE #4 FLOPPY #5 FORMAT #6 WINDOWS
Answer: KEYBOARD

118. **Jumbles:** #1 MILD #2 FLOOD #3 CLOUDY #4 TWISTER #5 RAINFALL #6 PRESSURE
Answer: TROPICAL STORM

119. **Jumbles:** #1 BRASS #2 NOTCH #3 FUSION #4 LETTER #5 DELUXE #6 MAGPIE
Answer: #1 SITCOM #2 SEINFELD

120. **Jumbles:** #1 PARKA #2 SCARF #3 FABRIC #4 BLOUSE #5 JUMPER #6 SNEAKER
Answer: PAJAMAS

121. **Jumbles:** #1 HONEY #2 DANISH #3 GARLIC #4 PRETZEL #5 OATMEAL #6 POPCORN
Answer: SPAGHETTI

122. **Jumbles:** #1 DINNER #2 CANCEL #3 DOLLAR #4 STIGMA #5 PRIMATE #6 CONTROL
Answer: #1 ISLAND #2 ICELAND #3 ATLANTIC

123. **Jumbles:** #1 RELAX #2 ROUGH #3 ROUND #4 REVISE #5 REPEAT #6 RANDOM #7 REGULAR #8 RAINBOW
Answer: RAILROAD

124. **Jumbles:** #1 FIVE ÷ FIVE = ONE
#2 SEVEN − FIVE = TWO
#3 FOUR + FOUR = EIGHT
#4 EIGHT x TWO = SIXTEEN
#5 TEN + TWENTY = THIRTY
Answer: ONE + ONE = FIVE − THREE

125. **Jumbles:** #1 HELMET #2 WEAPON #3 COPILOT #4 GUNBOAT #5 BLOCKADE #6 ARTILLERY
Answer: PURPLE HEART

126. **Jumbles:** #1 YEAST #2 MIMIC #3 MARGIN #4 NUANCE #5 WARMTH #6 GUESSED
Answer: #1 AWARD #2 GRAMMY #3 MUSICIAN

127. **Jumbles:** #1 ECHO #2 EVENT #3 USUAL #4 ADAPT #5 AGENDA #6 UPROAR #7 OUTCRY #8 ASPIRIN
Answer: APPETITE

128. **Jumbles:** #1 SUBWAY #2 VENDING #3 BERMUDA #4 RICKSHAW #5 AUSTRALIA
Answer: MARK TWAIN

129. **Jumbles:** #1 THE FIRM #2 THE MASK #3 SCARFACE #4 THE MUMMY #5 BRAVEHEART #6 GOODFELLAS
Answer: GHOSTBUSTERS

130. **Jumbles:** #1 EGG #2 WELL #3 ALLOW #4 REJECT #5 ICEBERG #6 BROCCOLI #7 HOROSCOPE #8 BASKETBALL #9 PUBLICATION #10 ENCYCLOPEDIA
Answer: CONSTELLATION

131. **Jumbles:** #1 MICHIGAN #2 DELAWARE #3 LOUISIANA #4 WISCONSIN #5 TENNESSEE #6 CALIFORNIA
Answer: WASHINGTON
Trivia Answer: VERMONT

132. **Jumbles:** #1 TYLER #2 TAYLOR #3 HOOVER #4 CLINTON #5 HARRISON #6 COOLIDGE
Answer: CLEVELAND
Trivia Answer: JOHN ADAMS

133. **Jumbles:** #1 PILOT #2 BUTLER #3 REALTOR #4 MUSICIAN #5 MECHANIC #6 CONDUCTOR
Answer: POLICEMAN

134. **Jumbles:** #1 POLKA #2 GUITAR #3 SONATA #4 PICCOLO #5 BASSOON #6 MANDOLIN
Answer: CLASSICAL

135. **Jumbles:** #1 ITALY #2 FRANCE #3 GREECE #4 POLAND #5 SWEDEN #6 BELGIUM #7 PORTUGAL
Answer: AUSTRIA

136. **Jumbles:** #1 BLACK #2 BOXER #3 DODGE #4 WIDTH #5 HIATUS #6 PARTNER
Answer: #1 BARK #2 BRANCH #3 REDWOOD

137. **Jumbles:** #1 FACTOR #2 NUMBER #3 ALGEBRA #4 FORMULA #5 INFINITY #6 POSITIVE
Answer: GEOMETRY

138. **Jumbles:** #1 CHEST #2 ANKLE #3 PELVIS #4 KIDNEY #5 THORAX #6 STOMACH
Answer: CLAVICLE

139. **Jumbles:** #1 LANSING #2 LINCOLN #3 HARTFORD #4 RICHMOND #5 COLUMBIA #6 FRANKFURT
Answer: HARRISBURG

140. **Jumbles:** #1 GIFT DONATION #2 PICKLE PROBLEM #3 RARING ANXIOUS #4 LAUNCH BLASTOFF #5 DISORDER CONFUSION
Answer: LAND ACREAGE

141. **Jumbles:** #1 DYNASTY #2 BONANZA #3 MATLOCK #4 JEOPARDY #5 THE ROOKIES #6 THE LOVE BOAT
Answer: DANIEL BOONE

142. **Jumbles:** #1 ISOBAR #2 THUNDER #3 CYCLONE #4 RAINBOW #5 MONSOON #6 PRESSURE
Answer: WEATHER MAP

143. **Jumbles:** #1 HOG #2 TURF #3 DITCH #4 OUTLAW #5 THOUGHT #6 FOOTBALL #7 MOUTHWASH #8 HORIZONTAL #9 SUPERMARKET #10 ABBREVIATION
Answer: UNCOMFORTABLE

144. **Jumbles:** #1 WARM FRIGID #2 HUSKY SCRAWNY #3 DECEIT HONESTY #4 VALLEY MOUNTAIN #5 POSITIVE NEGATIVE
Answer: WIDE NARROW

145. **Jumbles:** #1 ABYSS #2 GULCH #3 GLOBE #4 GROUND #5 CLIMATE #6 PLATEAU
Answer: ATMOSPHERE

146. **Jumbles:** #1 IRON #2 UNIFY #3 IMAGE #4 OUNCE #5 AWARD #6 OBJECT #7 OCCUPY #8 ABOLISH
Answer: INCREASE

147. **Jumbles:** #1 MEMENTO #2 DIE HARD #3 VACATION #4 HOOSIERS #5 MAGNOLIA #6 TOMBSTONE
Answer: DELIVERANCE

148. **Jumbles:** #1 TY COBB #2 CAL RIPKIN #3 YOGI BERRA #4 STEFFI GRAF #5 JOE MONTANA #6 TED WILLIAMS
Answer: TIGER WOODS

149. **Jumbles:** #1 HOMER #2 GOALIE #3 DEFEAT #4 SEASON #5 VICTORY #6 MANAGER
Answer: SCRIMMAGE

150. **Jumbles:** #1 PURGE #2 TUMMY #3 PROPER #4 COLUMN #5 PORTION #6 MEANING
Answer: #1 EUROPE #2 COUNTRY #3 PORTUGAL

151. **Jumbles:** #1 VAULT #2 MONEY #3 BANKER #4 CHARGE #5 DOLLAR #6 INCOME
Answer: REVENUE

152. **Jumbles:** #1 GEHRIG #2 SALMON #3 POTATOES #4 AVALANCHE #5 TORNADOES
Answer: SINGAPORE

153. **Jumbles:** #1 ROCKY #2 HOFFA #3 GHOST #4 DUMBO #5 TARZAN #6 MISERY
Answer: DIRTY HARRY

154. **Jumbles:** #1 TWO PLUS SEVEN = NINE #2 ONE PLUS THREE = FOUR #3 TWO TIMES FOUR = EIGHT #4 TWENTY MINUS TEN = TEN #5 THREE TIMES THREE = NINE
Answer: ONE PLUS EIGHT = NINE

155. **Jumbles:** #1 BOMB #2 CLASH #3 CHOPPER #4 WARSHIP #5 INFANTRY #6 CONFLICT
Answer: HIROSHIMA

156. **Jumbles:** #1 MODEST #2 GLOOMY #3 NATURAL #4 CHILDISH #5 SPACIOUS #6 SENSELESS
Answer: MONUMENTAL

157. **Jumbles:** #1 LYNX #2 RHINO #3 PANDA #4 BOBCAT #5 MUSKRAT #6 ELEPHANT
Answer: ARMADILLO
Trivia Answer: MANATEE

158. **Jumbles:** #1 CELERY #2 WAFFLE #3 TOMATO #4 LASAGNA #5 EGGPLANT #6 SANDWICH
Answer: CASSEROLE

159. **Jumbles:** #1 URANUS #2 PLANET #3 COSMOS #4 NEPTUNE #5 MERCURY #6 ASTRONOMY
Answer: SOLAR SYSTEM

160. **Jumbles:** #1 BELIEF #2 FIGURE #3 FUNNEL #4 COLLECT #5 SUPPORT #6 DWINDLE
Answer: #1 OFFICE #2 ELECTION #3 PRESIDENT

161. **Jumbles:** #1 FINCH #2 EAGLE #3 GOOSE #4 PIGEON #5 TURKEY #6 OSTRICH
Answer: PEACOCK

162. **Jumbles:** #1 CHILE #2 FINLAND #3 SOMALIA #4 HUNGARY #5 MOROCCO #6 PORTUGAL
Answer: MONGOLIA
Trivia Answers: #1 POLAND #2 AUSTRALIA

163. **Jumbles:** #1 PET #2 HOUR #3 SENSE #4 BUFFET #5 OCTOPUS #6 SUNSHINE #7 COCKROACH #8 SKATEBOARD #9 HUMINGBIRD #10 CHEESEBURGER
Answer: CIRCUMFERENCE

164. **Jumbles:** #1 SLOTH #2 FERRET #3 JAGUAR #4 WEASEL #5 GIRAFFE #6 LEMMING
Answer: ANTEATER

165. **Jumbles:** #1 SWEDEN #2 NORWAY #3 ESTONIA #4 HUNGARY #5 ROMANIA #6 SLOVAKIA #7 PORTUGAL
Answer: LITHUANIA

166. **Jumbles:** #1 DRAFT #2 ATTACK #3 CANTEEN #4 SAMURAI #5 GARRISON #6 DESTROYER
Answer: DESERT STORM

167. **Jumbles:** #1 BUYER #2 BADGE #3 GLOBAL #4 MODIFY #5 LATERAL #6 SHUTTER
Answer: #1 ATHLETE #2 BASEBALL #3 YOGI BERRA

168. **Jumbles:** #1 HILL #2 CREEK #3 ISLAND #4 VALLEY #5 JUNGLE #6 TUNDRA
Answer: AVALANCHE

169. **Jumbles:** #1 TWO SQUARED = FOUR #2 FOUR PLUS FOUR = EIGHT #3 NINE MINUS NINE = ZERO #4 SEVEN MINUS FIVE = TWO #5 THREE TIMES THREE = NINE
Answer: ONE MINUS FOUR = NEGATIVE THREE

170. **Jumbles:** #1 MOM #2 EXIT #3 HELLO #4 BIKINI #5 MASSIVE #6 SHOULDER #7 BOOKSHELF #8 WEATHERMAN #9 ADVERTISING #10 THUNDERSTORM
Answer: UNFORGETTABLE

171. **Jumbles:** #1 HOOD #2 TRUNK #3 HUBCAP #4 VEHICLE #5 CHASSIS #6 BATTERY #7 MILEAGE #8 IGNITION #9 ODOMETER
Answer: OIL CHANGE

172. **Jumbles:** #1 INNING #2 TENNIS #3 BOXING #4 HOCKEY #5 FUMBLE #6 DEFENSE #7 CATCHER #8 STADIUM #9 BASEBALL
Answer: BADMINTON

173. **Jumbles:** #1 HYENA #2 PANDA #3 KOALA #4 SHRIMP #5 WEASEL #6 PANTHER #7 MUSKRAT #8 WALLABY #9 ANTELOPE #10 KANGAROO
Answer: SALAMANDER

174. **Jumbles:** #1 CHEF #2 DEPUTY #3 BROKER #4 WAITER #5 WRITER #6 DOCTOR #7 JANITOR #8 CHEMIST #9 BUTCHER #10 MECHANIC
Answer: PHARMACIST

175. **Jumbles:** #1 GRAVY #2 FUDGE #3 HONEY #4 CELERY #5 LASAGNA #6 CRACKER #7 CUSTARD #8 COLESLAW #9 MEATBALL #10 SANDWICH
Answer: CHEESEBURGER

176. **Jumbles:** #1 ORBIT #2 PLUTO #3 COMET #4 GALAXY #5 SATURN #6 URANUS #7 JUPITER #8 NEPTUNE #9 MERCURY #10 ASTEROID
Answer: OUTER SPACE

177. **Jumbles:** #1 DAMP #2 SNOW #3 SUNNY #4 WINDY #5 HUMID #6 FREEZE #7 CLIMATE #8 TWISTER #9 DROUGHT #10 RAINFALL
Answer: THUNDERSTORM

178. **Jumbles:** #1 CAIRO #2 BERLIN #3 LISBON #4 HAVANA #5 LONDON #6 BOMBAY #7 WARSAW #8 TORONTO #9 MONTREAL #10 HONOLULU
Answer: BUENOS AIRES

Need More Jumbles?

Jumble® Books

More than 175 puzzles each!

Cowboy Jumble®
ISBN: 978-1-62937-355-3

Jammin' Jumble®
ISBN: 1-57243-844-4

Java Jumble®
ISBN: 978-1-60078-415-6

Jazzy Jumble®
ISBN: 978-1-57243-962-7

Jet Set Jumble®
ISBN: 978-1-60078-353-1

Joyful Jumble®
ISBN: 978-1-60078-079-0

Juke Joint Jumble®
ISBN: 978-1-60078-295-4

Jumble® Anniversary
ISBN: 987-1-62937-734-6

Jumble® at Work
ISBN: 1-57243-147-4

Jumble® Ballet
ISBN: 978-1-62937-616-5

Jumble® Birthday
ISBN: 978-1-62937-652-3

Jumble® Celebration
ISBN: 978-1-60078-134-6

Jumble® Circus
ISBN: 978-1-60078-739-3

Jumble® Cuisine
ISBN: 978-1-62937-735-3

Jumble® Drag Race
ISBN: 978-1-62937-483-3

Jumble® Ever After
ISBN: 978-1-62937-785-8

Jumble® Explorer
ISBN: 978-1-60078-854-3

Jumble® Explosion
ISBN: 978-1-60078-078-3

Jumble® Fever
ISBN: 1-57243-593-3

Jumble® Fiesta
ISBN: 1-57243-626-3

Jumble® Fun
ISBN: 1-57243-379-5

Jumble® Galaxy
ISBN: 978-1-60078-583-2

Jumble® Garden
ISBN: 978-1-62937-653-0

Jumble® Genius
ISBN: 1-57243-896-7

Jumble® Geography
ISBN: 978-1-62937-615-8

Jumble® Getaway
ISBN: 978-1-60078-547-4

Jumble® Gold
ISBN: 978-1-62937-354-6

Jumble® Grab Bag
ISBN: 1-57243-273-X

Jumble® Gymnastics
ISBN: 978-1-62937-306-5

Jumble® Jackpot
ISBN: 1-57243-897-5

Jumble® Jailbreak
ISBN: 978-1-62937-002-6

Jumble® Jambalaya
ISBN: 978-1-60078-294-7

Jumble® Jamboree
ISBN: 1-57243-696-4

Jumble® Jitterbug
ISBN: 978-1-60078-584-9

Jumble® Journey
ISBN: 978-1-62937-549-6

Jumble® Jubilation
ISBN: 978-1-62937-784-1

Jumble® Jubilee
ISBN: 1-57243-231-4

Jumble® Juggernaut
ISBN: 978-1-60078-026-4

Jumble® Junction
ISBN: 1-57243-380-9

Jumble® Jungle
ISBN: 978-1-57243-961-0

Jumble® Kingdom
ISBN: 978-1-62937-079-8

Jumble® Knockout
ISBN: 978-1-62937-078-1

Jumble® Madness
ISBN: 1-892049-24-4

Jumble® Magic
ISBN: 978-1-60078-795-9

Jumble® Marathon
ISBN: 978-1-60078-944-1

Jumble® Neighbor
ISBN: 978-1-62937-845-9

Jumble® Parachute
ISBN: 978-1-62937-548-9

Jumble® Safari
ISBN: 978-1-60078-675-4

Jumble® See & Search
ISBN: 1-57243-549-6

Jumble® See & Search 2
ISBN: 1-57243-734-0

Jumble® Sensation
ISBN: 978-1-60078-548-1

Jumble® Surprise
ISBN: 1-57243-320-5

Jumble® Symphony
ISBN: 978-1-62937-131-3

Jumble® Theater
ISBN: 978-1-62937-484-03

Jumble® University
ISBN: 978-1-62937-001-9

Jumble® Unleashed
ISBN: 978-1-62937-844-2

Jumble® Vacation
ISBN: 978-1-60078-796-6

Jumble® Wedding
ISBN: 978-1-62937-307-2

Jumble® Workout
ISBN: 978-1-60078-943-4

Jumpin' Jumble®
ISBN: 978-1-60078-027-1

Lunar Jumble®
ISBN: 978-1-60078-853-6

Monster Jumble®
ISBN: 978-1-62937-213-6

Mystic Jumble®
ISBN: 978-1-62937-130-6

Outer Space Jumble®
ISBN: 978-1-60078-416-3

Rainy Day Jumble®
ISBN: 978-1-60078-352-4

Ready, Set, Jumble®
ISBN: 978-1-60078-133-0

Rock 'n' Roll Jumble®
ISBN: 978-1-60078-674-7

Royal Jumble®
ISBN: 978-1-60078-738-6

Sports Jumble®
ISBN: 1-57243-113-X

Summer Fun Jumble®
ISBN: 1-57243-114-8

Touchdown Jumble®
ISBN: 978-1-62937-212-9

Travel Jumble®
ISBN: 1-57243-198-9

TV Jumble®
ISBN: 1-57243-461-9

Oversize Jumble® Books

More than 500 puzzles each!

Generous Jumble®
ISBN: 1-57243-385-X

Giant Jumble®
ISBN: 1-57243-349-3

Gigantic Jumble®
ISBN: 1-57243-426-0

Jumbo Jumble®
ISBN: 1-57243-314-0

The Very Best of Jumble® BrainBusters
ISBN: 1-57243-845-2

Jumble® Crosswords™

More than 175 puzzles each!

More Jumble® Crosswords™
ISBN: 1-57243-386-8

Jumble® Crosswords™ Jackpot
ISBN: 1-57243-615-8

Jumble® Crosswords™ Jamboree
ISBN: 1-57243-787-1

Jumble® BrainBusters™

More than 175 puzzles each!

Jumble® BrainBusters™
ISBN: 1-892049-28-7

Jumble® BrainBusters™ II
ISBN: 1-57243-424-4

Jumble® BrainBusters™ III
ISBN: 1-57243-463-5

Jumble® BrainBusters™ IV
ISBN: 1-57243-489-9

Jumble® BrainBusters™ 5
ISBN: 1-57243-548-8

Jumble® BrainBusters™ Bonanza
ISBN: 1-57243-616-6

Boggle™ BrainBusters™
ISBN: 1-57243-592-5

Boggle™ BrainBusters™ 2
ISBN: 1-57243-788-X

Jumble® BrainBusters™ Junior
ISBN: 1-892049-29-5

Jumble® BrainBusters™ Junior II
ISBN: 1-57243-425-2

Fun in the Sun with Jumble® BrainBusters™
ISBN: 1-57243-733-2